I Got The Job!

Craig DiVizzio

Copyright © 2020 by Craig DiVizzio

All rights reserved. No part of this publication may be reproduced, distributed, or transmitted in any form or by any means, including photocopying, recording, or using any other electronic or mechanical methods, without the prior written permission of the author, except in the case of brief quotations embodied in critical reviews and certain other noncommercial uses permitted by copyright law.

Any references to historical events, real people, or real places are used fictitiously.

Front cover image by Andrea Harrison and Heather Lee
Book design by Leigh Anne Hall

Thanks to DiVizzio International, your resource for top-shelf professional development eLearning courses, videos, eBooks, and audio books.

Let's Connect

www.craigdivizzio.com

www.perspectives.craigdivizzio.com

DiVizzio International on YouTube

DiVizzio International on Facebook

Craig DiVizzio on LinkedIn

WHY I WROTE THIS BOOK

Quarantined at home during the COVID-19 pandemic of 2020, I saw the news. Businesses were closing. People were losing their jobs, and unemployment numbers were through the roof. I saw those COVID-related graphs and predictions daily, and I realized that I know things that can really make a difference. You see, I have been teaching interviewing skills for decades, and I can't count the number of times former participants reached out to say, "Hey Craig, I got the job!"

I knew that if I could get my knowledge into a book or virtual course, I could help people just like you. So, I started writing.

They say that the first step in writing is to know your audience. Well, you are my audience. I know you have written an engaging resume, completed the application process, selected influential references, and done your networking and research. All this work resulted in an interview for a job you would love, and that prospect is both exciting and daunting. How do you best present yourself to win that job?

Believe it or not, anyone can be a great interviewee

once they know what to do and how to prepare properly.

In this book, you will learn what to say and do and what not to say and do.

When you take what you learn from this book and invest the time to prepare yourself, you can't help but be successful. Watch out, though. Investing the time and energy I'm going to recommend involves discipline. The effort can be time-consuming. To convince people that you are, indeed, the very best person for the job, you will need to know your message inside and out.

The reward for your preparation and practice is being selected for the position. The work you put into preparing for a great interview will change what you do, whom you do it with and for, and how you provide for yourself and your family. And that's a big deal!

Table of Contents

Preface: "Hey Craig, I Got the Job!" 7
Who Has the Advantage? 10
How to Handle Competition 12

1 Before The Interview 15
Interview Preparation: Recording Yourself 16
Typical Steps 19
References 20
What to Prepare 23
What Interviewers Look For 29
The No-Questions Interview 31
Highlighting Commonalities 34
Must-Say Items 36

2 Convincing The Interviewer 39
Selling Yourself 40
Separating Yourself from the Competition 44
Using Power Phrases 47
Speaking with Certainty 48

3 Answering Critical Questions 51
Tell Me about Yourself: The Opening Statement 52
Twenty-Second Opening 60
Why Should I Hire You? 61
Why Do You Want This Job? 63
Do You Have Anything You'd Like to Add? The Closing Statement 65
Twenty-Second Closing 70
Behavioral Answers 71
The STAR Method 76
Behavioral Categories and Trigger Words 81
The Weakness Questions: Turning Weaknesses into Strengths 83

4 Perfecting Your Answers 92

Designing Great Answers 93
Answering without Sounding Scripted 97

5 Last-Minute Matters 100

The Last Few Hours 101
Entrance and Exit 103
First Impressions 105
Meeting the Greeter 108

6 During The Interview 111

The Basics 112
Managing Your Nerves 120
Using Your Portfolio 129
Giving a Great Presentation 131

7 Special Situations 137

Selling Transferable Skills 138
Overcoming Overqualification 141
Deciding That You Don't Want the Job 148
Rejecting an Offer 150

8 After The Interview 152

Saying Thank You 153
Preparing for the Next Step 154

9 Other Interview Types 156

Internal Interviews 157
Virtual Interviews 160
Phone Interviews 164
Job Fair Interviews 166

10 Hey Craig, I Got The Job! 169

About the Author 171

One Last Thing 172

Preface: "Hey Craig, I Got the Job!"

Hi, I'm Craig DiVizzio, and while I hear that exclamation very often, helping someone find a fulfilling career never gets old. Welcome to the *I Got the Job!* interviewing system. In all my years of teaching and coaching, nothing has meant more to me than hearing someone say, "Craig, I got the job!" And you're already one step closer, so let's get to it.

You are in for an exciting journey, one that ends with you interviewing better than you ever have before. Here, condensed for your immediate access and quick learning, is what I have learned from conducting thousands of employment interviews over many years. While I believe that success is seldom convenient and that you've got your work cut out for you, you've already proven your dedication. That's why you purchased this book!

You may come to this course needing to get a job—any job—like yesterday! Or, you may be comfortably looking for the right job or the ideal job. The situation you seek may be similar to your last one or a complete change of direction. Regardless of your intent and current skill level, this book will prepare you to stand out from your competition.

Ideally, you can read this book from beginning to end, but if you have a specific interest or limited time, dive right into the section that will help you the most.

How important is an employment interview? Well, the outcome of the interview determines what work you will do, whom you do it with, where you do it, and how you will financially provide for yourself and your family. It will also determine whether you find your ideal job if that is what you are seeking.

You and I both know that life isn't always fair, right? Well, unfortunately, interviews aren't either. Interviewers may be untrained, unprepared, or biased. Sometimes they ask unfair and even unlawful questions. Sometimes, they talk and don't allow you to discuss your qualifications. The interview room may be poorly placed. It may be too small, drafty, stuffy, or near a high-traffic area. Interviews can be too long or too short. Sometimes, another candidate has already been selected. Regardless of the conditions, however, success rarely occurs without proper preparation. That's a hard truth.

This book gives you a step-by-step method of overcoming the negatives. We will cover proper preparation, how to convince the interviewer to hire you, how to answer the critical questions, and how to perfect your answers. By the time you greet the interviewer, you will know without a doubt that you have great answers. We are going to talk about what you must do hours before the interview, during the interview, and after the interview. And we will cover all the different types of interviews that you may need to prepare for during your job search.

If you follow the plan in this book, you will

- Be properly prepared
- Create memorable first and final impressions
- Know how to design engaging, informative answers
- Clearly and concisely articulate your answers
- Sell yourself to the interviewer
- Avoid common pitfalls
- Master the critical steps to having a successful interview

So, how important is an interview? Darned important! You spend over one half of your waking life at work, and that's a BIG deal. The *I Got the Job!* interviewing system can change your life! Let's get started.

Who Has the Advantage?

You may have heard people say that it's easier to find a job when you have a job. But is it?

If you are currently employed and searching for a new job solely for a more exciting or better opportunity, then you probably have financial peace of mind. This peace of mind can give you leverage in the interview. You don't have to accept just any opportunity. You can wait for the right job, in the right location, with the right benefits.

On the other hand, this same peace of mind can lead to poor motivation. If so, being currently employed will not work in your favor. I have interviewed many people with an overly casual attitude. It's easy to tell when a candidate thinks *Well, if I get this job, great. If I don't, it's no big deal. At least I have a job to go to tomorrow.* Believe me: the interviewer sees this lack of enthusiasm. On the other hand, hunger is a powerful motivator. Candidates who are hungry are energetic, and the interviewer(s) see this abundance of energy, too.

Often, a lack of motivation is a barrier to essential preparation. The employed person may prepare less fervently than the unemployed person. The employed person also faces the challenge of finding enough time to design answers and work on other interview prep tasks.

Those who are between jobs are typically hungry for work and highly motivated to prepare well. Certainly, if you are currently unemployed or underemployed, you face tremendous pressure to find a job. This pressure impacts your ability to find the perfect job because you need a job as soon as possible and don't have the time or resources to be selective.

Financial anxiety, the stress of unemployment, the pressure of the job search, and the feeling that you are out of sync with the world, and the structure of work can cause desperation and over-eagerness. Hide these feelings when you go into the interview. Interviewers prefer confidence, self-approval, calmness, and control to desperation.

So, is it easier to find a job when you are working?

Is it easier to find a job when you're working?
Who cares?

Maybe or maybe not. My answer is *who cares?* Worrying about whether you have an advantage or disadvantage isn't going to change your situation.

Don't focus on the things that might limit you. Instead, commit to managing any obstacles and capitalizing on everything that you've got going for you. If your singular focus is preparing to do your absolute best, you will be fine!

How to Handle Competition

How long has it been since you have faced some real competition? Have you recently worked in a team-oriented environment where competition is discouraged? Have you worked in an environment that doesn't require or welcome innovation, creativity, or out-of-the-box thinking? Think about a time when you faced a challenge to get something you wanted. Get in touch with those emotions and put them to work.

NEWS FLASH—In today's climate, we are all flat out competing for the best jobs. I think you can safely assume that some of the people you are competing against may be more qualified than you. Your competitors may have been doing the work longer than you. Their list of accomplishments may be longer and more prestigious than yours. They may have worked in exciting cities with large, very visible companies. On paper, they may appear more qualified. But get this: What your competition looks like on paper DOES NOT matter!

Yes, you read that correctly; what your competitors look like on paper DOES NOT matter! You see, when people talk about who is most qualified, typically it's resume stuff. But the resume is just the beginning. Many things beyond the resume contribute to a hiring decision. If you got an interview, consider yourself qualified!

Now that you are qualified, what are the interviewer(s) looking for? They may wonder who will be easy to work with. They think about whether they like you. Would they enjoy hanging out with you? They imagine how you will fit with other team members. These human factors all contribute to the hiring decision just as much, and sometimes more than your resume qualifications.

Years and years of experience have taught me that you can quit worrying about who is the most qualified on paper. Instead, focus your time and energy on the interview preparation. There is no substitute for preparation. There is no short cut. You must do your absolute best in the interview. If you want to exponentially increase your chance of landing your ideal job, prioritize your time and prepare, prepare, prepare.

Begin your preparation by expecting to compete against only the top-ranked candidates. Let's talk about what you must do to prepare well and win this competition. You know you can do this!

～ 1 ～

BEFORE THE INTERVIEW

You might as well know from the very beginning that I believe in preparation. I believe in practice. There is no other way to really make an impact in an interview except by extensive preparation. Yes, this is going to take some time, but it will be worth it when you find that job that is a good match for your interests and abilities. Let's get started.

Interview Preparation: Recording Yourself

I've got a question for you. Have you ever video recorded yourself when preparing for an interview? If not, then you are missing out on a huge opportunity, but you aren't alone.

Photo by *Rodrigo Souza* from *Pexels*

When you record yourself, you will learn several things that will help you more than you can imagine when you get to the interview. I know it's a pain to set up a cell phone or camera, sit down, and then try to replicate interviewing in front of two or three people. Right off the bat, it requires additional preparation. Next, it requires you to make "eye contact" around an empty room. You must say and do everything that you would say or do in an actual interview, and this just feels weird. Besides, you just don't like seeing yourself on video. Most people won't prepare this much. Do you want to succeed? Then don't let any of these things stop you! Now, let me tell you why video recording is the most critical interview prep task you can do. When you see yourself from the interviewer(s) perspective, you can identify both your mistakes and your strengths.

Obviously, when you see your mistakes, you can correct them well before the interview. But imagine this: when you see what you do well, you learn where you should keep doing what you're doing. Not only will you avoid

> ## *Imagine This*
> When you see what you are doing well, you can keep yourself aligned with your natural strengths.

wasting precious preparation time, but you will also be able to keep yourself and your presentation aligned with your natural strengths.

Did you hear that? I said that you can avoid over-preparing in areas where you are already strong. I almost never tell anyone that they can spend less time in preparation. Why would I say such a thing?

In an interview, people tend to get rigid and strive to have all the perfect answers. For an interviewer, the best part of the meeting is that moment when the candidate is just up there flying. This is when they are energetic, in their comfort zone, and exuding lots of energy and enthusiasm. Those are beautiful moments.

Unfortunately, many people reign themselves in and repeat their memorized answers. My concern is that over practicing may guide you away from your natural passion and presence. Video recording yourself will allow you to see what works, what doesn't, and where rigidity has set in.

As you video record yourself, try putting pictures of your friends nearby so you can get in the habit of making eye contact around the room. Look at the pictures when you speak. Speak directly to your friend's picture, using his or her name each time.

You've probably heard that people like the sound of their own names. But did you know that the peer-reviewed journal *ScienceDirect* published a study on the topic? You can find it on the National Institute of Health website. The study used functional MRIs to measure how people reacted to hearing their own first names among other first names. When people heard their own names, three regions in the left hemisphere of the brain were activated. The researchers concluded that "hearing one's own name creates unique brain functioning."[1] All that to

---

[1] Carmody, Dennis P, and Michael Lewis. "Brain Activation When Hearing One's Own and Others' Names." *Brain Research*, U.S. National Library of Medicine, 20 Oct. 2006.

say that research concluded what we already knew. People like hearing their own names. Do you think it's worth the effort to use people's names? Darn right, it is! We'll dig into this more later.

After you video record yourself, be easy on yourself as you watch it. Write down the things that need improvement and write down what you're doing well. Don't stop with one recording. Do this exercise several times over a short period: record, watch, notice mistakes and strengths. Soon, you'll be able to compare two, three, or four videos. When you watch that fourth video right after you watch the first, you'll be amazed. Wow! You'll see the improvement after just a little work, and your confidence will soar.

This exercise really pays dividends when you walk into the actual interview. You will be confident because you know you have the right answers as well as the right delivery.

Typical Steps

In preparing for the interview, you'll face some typical hurdles. You may fill out an application, and the application may require references. You may have to go online and record some answers. You may have a virtual interview through Zoom, FaceTime, GoToMeeting, or another platform. You may have a phone interview. Eventually, you'll have a face-to-face interview.

This book focuses on face-to-face interviews because these are the most difficult. We will capture all interview types with slight modifications for these other situations.

One of the steps above is providing references, so let's talk about what makes a great reference.

References

What's the difference between an okay reference and an excellent reference? First and most importantly, your reference should be somebody who knows you well and believes you are outstanding. Would you rather your reference say, *They're pretty good* or, *They're the best that you can hire*!

If you can, choose someone who has credibility in the company—someone who is generally admired.

Another excellent choice is someone who has

credibility with the hiring manager. When a hiring manager respects and values a person's opinion, they begin to associate your name with that same value. When the other interviewer(s) hear the hiring manager discuss you in this way, your value automatically increases. Be careful, though. There is a sticky point in using a reference who has a close relationship with the hiring manager. Your reference must be somebody who knows you and your work well, not a recent or casual acquaintance. If your reference doesn't know you well, you're just name dropping.

Another excellent choice is someone who will be eager to help. When you ask this person if they would serve as your reference, you want to hear, *Absolutely! I want to help in any way I can.* A person who wants to help is willing to put their name next to yours. They're willing to risk their reputation based on your performance! They really believe in you.

Finally, because your references will be communicating either in writing or through conversation, they must be outstanding communicators.

Now, let's assume that you have a list of possible references with several excellent choices. Your list includes people who know your work and believe it to be outstanding. These same people are well respected at the company, and you even have some people who are valued by the hiring manager. If everything else is truly equal, choose the person who holds the highest position in the company.

Did you know that there are two different ways to handle references? Most people only use the passive option. When using the passive method, you give reference names to the hiring manager or the HR department, and you hope that they choose to contact your references. Hope is nice, but it's not proactive.

I encourage you to choose a proactive approach to references. When you reach out to ask someone to be your reference, give them the name, number, and contact information for the hiring manager. Ask if they would be willing to make a call. If a phone call is impossible, ask if they would email or text the hiring manager with a positive word about you and your work performance. Being proactive gives you more control over the reference process. It also is the very best assurance that the hiring manager will hear good things about you before the interview.

Want to really take it to the next level? Consider asking your reference for feedback after their discussion with the hiring manager. Maybe you can learn which areas the hiring manager is focused on. Maybe something about your qualifications excited the hiring manager. With this inside information, you can use your interview to promote your skills in the specific areas most relevant to the job and most important to the hiring manager.

It's worth your time to think about your references. Choosing excellent references can make a big difference!

What to Prepare

Having taught interviewing for years and years and having interviewed thousands of people, I can confidently tell you that lack of preparation is the number one reason candidates don't land the job. You must do your research and prepare what to say and practice how to say it. Do you want the job? Then get prepared and stay prepared.

This is how you stay prepared. If you're in the process of interviewing for several jobs, you may have an interview this week and another one in a month or two. During the interim, continuously review your answers. Imagine being confidently prepared when a headhunter calls and says, "Hey, are you available for an interview? Sorry about the late notice, but the schedule is for tomorrow."

Get prepared and stay prepared because short-notice interviews really happen. Being prepared eliminates stress. Remember the old saying: The early bird gets the worm.

You'll get prepared by digging into some research. First, learn everything you can about the job itself, the company, the department, the team, the person you would report to, and that person's position within the company. You must also learn about the interview process and the type of interview platform the company uses. Some companies provide all this information in the job posting, but others only include job responsibilities and basic company information. It's your task to understand everything about whatever level of information the company provides. If you are patient, creative, and dig deep, you can often find the information you seek by searching the Internet and making some phone calls.

Understanding the job requirements is a fundamental and frequent interview question: *Tell me how you understand the position responsibilities.* You would be surprised how many candidates don't give a clear answer to this simple question. Since the answers are in the job description, you must answer this question well. Candidates who don't have a clear answer send a mixed message. They want the job, but they don't understand what the job is. Prepare to answer this question, and you'll be in a good position to tackle the harder ones.

Interview situations vary, so it's okay to question whoever is setting up the meeting. Let's look at different types of interviews and the questions that can eliminate surprises on interview day.

Question 1

What does the interview process entail? A big mistake people make is assuming that everybody—even persons within the same company—will use the same interview process. Don't just rely on past information. If you are interviewing with a company where you had a previous interview, you may find the process and interview platform to be completely different.

See if you can learn if a telephone interview precedes a face-to-face interview. Try to find out with whom you will interview. What is their job title? What is their department's mission?

Question 2

What is the interview platform? Often, the first interview is a telephone interview. Increasingly, you may have an initial virtual interview through Facetime, Zoom, Skype, or another platform. Sometimes, you'll face sequential interviews. Sequential interviews allow you to meet a variety of people quickly. You'll have an interview, finish it, go to another interview, finish it, and go to another. Panel interviews are very common. In these, several people will interview you at the same time. Some of these people will be potential co-workers, one may be the hiring manager, one may be from human resources, and one may be another supervisor.

Question 3

How many people will be on the panel? If you do have a panel interview, you'll want to learn how many people to expect. Many candidates have been surprised by the number of people in the room. Imagine expecting one or two people, opening the door, and seeing seven! It can throw you, and sometimes candidates don't gather their confidence until the interview is almost over.

Think about these remaining questions. What benefits will you gain from learning the answers ahead of time?

Question 4

How many interviews will occur before an offer is extended?

Question 5

Approximately how much time is allotted for the interview?

Question 6

Is there anything in particular that the hiring manager would like for me to prepare?

Question 7

How many questions will they ask?

Question 8

What's the proper dress code?

Question 9

Generally, how long does the company take to decide? Now, why is that important? When you're looking for a job, you are probably interviewing at more than one company. You may have five interviews this week. Knowing when the company will make a decision will help you accept the best offer, for the best job. Asking the right questions and having enough information will provide you that leverage. Sometimes, especially if the labor market is tight, the interviewer may ask if you are actively interviewing with other companies. They also want to make a decision quickly, especially if you are a strong candidate.

Do your preparation! Do your research! Once you know the company and you have all the relevant information, it's time to prepare for the interview. Practice clearly articulating your answers and video record your mock interview several times. At this point, you will have spent at least 60 hours preparing for the interview. After you've prepared for a couple of interviews, you may find that the preparation for subsequent interviews is less labor-intensive. Trust me: the time goes by very quickly.

You know that feeling—the one that tells you that you could have done better. You don't want to feel that feeling. Don't miss out on a dream job because you didn't do your best. If you do find yourself thinking that you could have done better if you had researched a little bit more or spent a little bit more time practicing, then admit it: Craig was right. Learn from the experience and self-correct.

Your objective is to go into the interview and do your absolute best. You cannot control how the company selects a candidate, but you can manage your performance.

 How great does it feel to leave the interview thinking, *That's as good as it gets! I gave it my best.* Now, that's the indicator of proper preparation!

What Interviewers Look For

People often ask me, *Craig, what do interviewers look for?* Here are the top six winning interview components.

1. Interviewers need to know that you attempted to talk with the hiring manager before the interview, so make sure to communicate this information. What is the value of doing that? If you spoke with the hiring manager, you were able to ask questions. You learned what characteristics the hiring manager values and which qualifications are the most important. You even found out whether you like the hiring manager. Even if you attempted to speak with the hiring manager, but were unsuccessful, share that. Taking this step is viewed positively, and it's worth sharing. It shows that you did your homework to prepare well for the interview.

2. Interviewers look for a professional appearance. However, every company does not define professional appearance equally. Find out what the company considers professional attire or appropriate for the interview.

3. Interviewers want a personal connection with the candidate. Build rapport with the interviewer(s). Make a connection with them. Use eye contact, address people by name, and speak directly with each interviewer over the course of your answers.

4. Interviewers look for confident communicators. As you answer questions, don't say *you know* or *I uh*. Avoid slang phrases and filler words.

Prepare and present a great opening statement that's about 1 – 2 minutes long. The opening statement should be the very first information you share. When responding to questions, thoroughly answer the questions, and give good examples. You'll learn how to craft an opening statement and great answers later in this book.

5. Interviewers want to see your enthusiasm for the job. The number one comment employers make about unsuccessful candidates is that they did not sell themselves. Sell yourself. Hint: You will need to prepare how to this before the interview.

6. Ask the interviewer(s) great questions and present a good closing statement.

These are the things most interviewers look for, and we will cover them all.

The No-Questions Interview

When preparing for the interview, prepare an agenda. Does that seem odd? Doesn't the interviewer run the meeting? Yes and no. The interviewer has an agenda and may or may not have prepared properly. Are you going to let someone's agenda and quality of preparation impact how you sell yourself? Of course not.

You also have an agenda. You want the interviewer(s) to learn all the best information about you. Get that information on paper. Doing so will require you to develop a picture of yourself. Once you have that, then decide how to communicate this picture to the interviewer(s).

Just like when you create a profile on LinkedIn, developing your interview profile requires you to become reacquainted with your skills, knowledge, and education.

The next step is to help the interviewer(s) connect the dots between your assets and the job requirements. You must be able to discuss this connection knowledgeably.

I encourage you to prepare for an interview where the

interviewer(s) ask absolutely no questions. I used this interview format when I was a department head at a college. Candidates would come to the interview expecting interview questions, but I didn't ask any. I would say, "I don't have any questions for you, but I would like for you to use the next 30 to 40 minutes to tell me everything you want me to know about you. Convince me to hire you."

How long do you think people talked when they had not prepared for that type of interview? Would you believe three or four minutes? They had no idea what to tell me. To their detriment, they had relied on interview questions to help them along. Was it easy for me to create a shortlist of the best candidates? You bet.

To prepare for a no-question interview, evaluate what you bring to the table. What about your work history and personal background makes you the ideal candidate? Think about your education, your specific skills, your knowledge, and your experiences. Discussing your goals, and even what you think about leadership is relevant and appropriate. Once you've thought of everything that you want the interviewer(s) to know, organize the information logically. Connect the dots between the job requirements and your profile.

To start organizing, take a sheet of paper and divide it into two columns. List all the things that you identified about your profile in the left column and all the things the job requires in the right. Now, match them up. When you're done, you can confidently say that what you bring meets or exceeds the job requirements.

Of course, you'll have to tidy up that brainstorming exercise when you write your agenda. But now you know exactly how to help the interviewer(s) see you as the perfect candidate. You'll show the interviewer(s) how you have already met the challenges of this job in your previous experience. For example, you may say, *I know this job requires a high aptitude. I have demonstrated high aptitude in the following ways . . .* All you're doing is connecting the dots. With this preparation, you'll weave your life experiences into the job responsibilities. Now you have a convincing narrative of the value you bring to the company.

The following list should help you begin brainstorming.
- Background
- Skills
- Education
- Experiences
- Knowledge
- Goals
- Safety
- Values

- Achievements
- Leadership
- Teamwork
- Diversity
- Why this job?
- Why now?

Highlighting Commonalities

Earlier, I suggested that you should look for things you have in common with the interviewer(s). Remember when we discussed rapport? A great way to build rapport is to find commonalities. It's human nature to like people with whom we have something in common.

When you get together with a friend, what do you talk about? Do you talk to each other about people the other doesn't know? What about hobbies that the other doesn't enjoy? I have an acquaintance that does this. I promise you it's a boring conversation. I cringe when I see his name pop up on my phone. When you converse with a true friend, I'm almost certain that you talk about things you have in common.

Have you ever met somebody for the first time, and after chatting for a bit, you find that their preferences are just different from yours? You don't connect on any of the answers. What kind of music do you like? What do you enjoy doing on vacation? What types of movies do you go to? Nothing connects. You move on, looking for someone with whom you connect.

When we find commonalities, people tend to like us a little bit more. Of course, when you find a commonality with an interviewer, you'll need to make it relevant to the job. For example, I used this one when interviewing for a corporate trainer position.

I have been riding motorcycles for 40 years. When I learned that one of the interviewers also rides, I said, "Bill, you'll understand this answer because I know you ride a motorcycle also. This business can be extremely demanding. Now and then, I need to push away from it, de-stress, and refresh so that when I come back into the classroom or studio, I am ready to do my best. One of the best ways for me to take a mental break, to step away from my business, is to ride my motorcycle. Riding my motorcycle as a hobby makes me a more focused trainer. It gives me the downtime that I need to come back to work with renewed energy." Using this personal connection, I was able to capitalize on something that the interviewer and I share, while at the same time making it relevant to how the hobby makes me a better trainer.

Find commonalities, if you can, by doing your research. You'll be surprised what you can learn online if you are patient and tenacious. Find a way to make these commonalities relevant. Then share those answers. You will find that people connect with you and like you a little bit more. And that's exactly what we want when we leave the interview!

Must-Say Items

Once you have prepared your body of information for the no-question interview, you'll see that some items stand out. These are your must-say items. The must-say items are the critical information that the interviewer(s) must hear about you. Must-say items are your most significant selling points. It doesn't matter if the interviewer(s) are asking for them. They need to know. Choose four or five items, list them in the middle of the top sheet of paper in your portfolio, and title them *Must-Say*.

Only choose four or five because it's difficult to share more than five. During the interview, listen for places to bring them up. When you talk about one, cross it off.

The beautiful part of this system is that you can always make an opportunity to speak to everything on the list. This way, you will tell the interviewer(s) everything you want them to know.

> *You can make an opportunity to speak to everything on your must-say list!*

When the interviewer(s) exhaust all their questions, typically the last item they ask will be, *Do you have anything else you want to say before we end?* Let's imagine that you have one or two must-say items left. You should respond, *as a matter of fact, there were a couple of things I want to tell you that I haven't shared yet.* Then, you cover those final two items and move immediately into your closing statement.

When you've crossed everything off the list, you will know that you gave them your best stuff. You'll know that if it wasn't good enough, that's okay. You'll be cool with not being hired because it's probably not the right job for you.

Whatever you do, don't carry your best stuff out the door and then nag yourself with a list of regrets. When you check that list off and walk out with confidence, you'll know that you gave them your very best. More importantly, you'll know that it is going to be enough!

~ 2 ~

CONVINCING THE INTERVIEWER

Your number one objective when walking into an interview is to be convincing—to convince them to hire you. My question to you is this: In general conversation, how persuasive are you? Let's talk about this in-depth because there are several things you should know about how to be convincing. The first one is selling yourself. Let's check it out.

Selling Yourself

In an interview, you must sell yourself. The most common feedback candidates who didn't get hired hear is, *you didn't sell yourself to us*. Unfortunately, many people have a hard time saying *I'm the best person for this job, and here is the reason why*. Let's dig into exactly how to sell yourself—how to tell your story. When you tell your story, the story will show the interviewer(s) just how good you are.

Are you unsure about how to sell yourself without coming across as arrogant or boastful? Don't worry, certain magic words can endow your story with appreciation and humility, even while you are conveying why you are the best candidate for the position. Before we get into how to tell your story, let's talk about where to find your story.

You have many experiences that can be turned into a story. How do you find the best experiences for your interview? Think about what you can quantify—what you can count. Data helps the interviewer(s) assign value to your accomplishments. Data helps you point to accomplishments with evidence and validity. Because people tend to trust numbers, data doesn't come across as boastful. Instead, you are simply stating facts. Use raw numbers, ratios, or percentages to quantify your story.

But data alone is boring. For your story to be compelling, it needs more than data. Where can you find a story like that? What experiences make a great story? Consider those times where you were selected or chosen. Think of times you were chosen for a special project that resulted in quantifiable success. Maybe you were chosen to solve a problem or improve efficiency. Think about times when people believed in you and had confidence that you were the right person to manage an important task to completion. Of course, also think about times when you were awarded or rewarded for something.

The first step in crafting your story is recalling and writing down all these experiences. The next step is choosing some specific words to include in your story. When you tell a story about your success, you straddle a fine line between being perceived as arrogant and conceited or being perceived as the best person for the job.

The following words are magic.

They allow you to sell yourself without causing any misperceptions of arrogance.

Magic Words

Appreciate	**Privilege**	
"I appreciated..."	"It was a privilege to..."	
Grateful	**Fortunate**	**Rewarding**
"I am grateful to have been able to..."	"I have been very fortunate to have..."	"It was a rewarding experience when..."
Honor	**Humbling**	
"It was an honor to..."	"It was a humbling experience to be chosen to..."	

Here are some magic words: appreciate, fortunate, grateful, honor, humbling, privilege, rewarding. Arrogant or conceited people rarely use words like these. You may begin your story like this, *I was very fortunate in my career to...* As the interviewer(s) listen, these magic words will help them focus on the story instead of questioning your personality traits. Practice using these magic words in daily conversation and make sure to include them when you tell your story.

Here's an example of how to use the magic words. Back in 1996, the Olympics were in Atlanta, GA, where I live. The Olympians became top athletes, first on their college team, then on the national team, and finally on the Olympic team. But, after the Olympics were over, these elite athletes had to completely change their focus. They needed jobs.

For many Olympic athletes, finding a job would be a new experience. They needed to learn how to write a resume, how to network, and how to interview. To help the athletes transition, the Olympic Committee hosted workshops as appreciation for the athletes' participation in the Olympics.

Since I was a trainer who had frequently taught this information, I really wanted to be a part of these workshops. Who wouldn't want to train 22 Olympic athletes surrounded by the pomp and circumstance of the event? Who wouldn't want to stand in front of Olympic banners and share information with a group of exceptionally motivated and accomplished people? I am grateful to have been chosen out of 200 trainers for this position. And I cannot begin to convey how rewarding and humbling the experience was. It was one of the most memorable times of my career!

Notice that in my story, I didn't once say that I was good at what I do. However, the listener immediately understands that being chosen to do that work indicates that I am well qualified. That's how you sell yourself!

Separating Yourself from the Competition

Interviewers who have interviewed several people in a day sometimes find that they have selected candidates with many of the same hard and soft skill sets. Now, they must choose the best candidate from very similar, very qualified people. It's a familiar and frustrating challenge for seasoned interviewers.

Because the candidates can seem so similar to the interviewer(s), you must distinguish yourself from the

Photo by Jessica Ruscello on Unsplash¶

competition. Only you can differentiate yourself from the group of suitable candidates. Only you can convince the interviewer(s) that you are the best candidate.

I suggest you separate yourself from the competition as early as possible in the interview. If you can accomplish this, the interviewer(s) will see you as different and better than the competition throughout the whole interview. Since they already perceive you to be superior, they will listen to what you say more closely.

Setting yourself apart in this way may seem daunting. How do you make it happen? You separate yourself from competitors by presenting your uniqueness. You have unique knowledge and experiences, and this individuality makes you shine. During your interview preparation, brainstorm, and get this unique knowledge and experience on paper. Next, assess which items represent your most significant value. Now, when you get to the interview, share those things that make you who you are—those things that are distinctive to what you know and how you can contribute. Show the interviewer(s) that you are the best candidate for the job.

Unique traits could include a rare or desired strength, a character trait, or a combination of skills that stand out. Maybe you worked on a project that sets you apart because other candidates may not have had the same level of responsibility. Perhaps you have an unusual or different perspective on work-life because of your life opportunities or previous work experiences.

When you share individual experiences with the interviewer(s), call attention to them. For example, you might preface your comments with an attention-getter like, *I'm a little bit different than others you may see today.* Now, you are ready to thoughtfully present your unique self!

Do you need some help finding your most valuable assets? Check out the job description. Included are minimum qualifications and preferred qualifications. Required skillsets, education, experience, knowledge, and certifications are examples of minimum qualifications. Preferred qualifications are above and beyond the minimum requirements.

For example, the job description might read, *Five years of experience in a progressive human resources role is required. Professional Human Resources (PHR) certification is preferred.* The company expects candidates to have the minimum qualification of five years of HR experience. The PHR is preferred. Not having the certification won't necessarily limit your opportunity for an interview. Having some or all of the preferred qualifications is a definite plus. These preferred qualifications are a great way to distinguish yourself from the competition.

> You must cover these areas of individuality in the interview, reinforcing that you are the best candidate for the job!

Try this: Mention your preferred qualifications in your opening statement, in your closing statement, and when you discuss why they should hire you. This reinforcement will further separate you from your competitors!

Using Power Phrases

Another interviewing skill that directly impacts your opportunity to convince the interviewer(s) is speaking in power phrases. Power phrases are phrases spoken with certainty—words that are impactful and not easily misinterpreted. An example of a power phrase is, *there is no doubt in my mind*. There is no doubt. It is certain, specific, and not mistaken. I encourage you to highlight those words with emphasis as you speak them:

- I am convinced that . . .
- I assure you that . . .
- I am confident that . . .
- I take great pride in . . .
- I have been extremely successful doing . . .

You will come up with more of your own power phrases. Practice speaking the power phrases, so they just roll off your tongue—until they are a natural part of your overall communication.

Make a list of the most impactful things that you can say in the interview.

Next, decide where to use them throughout the interview. Be careful, though. Make sure that you use them effectively without overusing them.

Your opening statement is a good place for a power phrase. Use one more in your closing statement. When you are asked, *Why should we hire you,* use at least one power phrase.

Power phrases cause the interviewer(s) to view you as confident, mature, articulate, and overall, the best candidate.

Speaking with Certainty

Next in importance to using power phrases is speaking with certainty.

How do you speak with certainty? You avoid certain words, and you include other words. Avoid words or statements that are vague, ambiguous, doubtful, or uncertain. For example, don't say, *I hope.* I hope sounds uncertain—as if you can't even convince yourself. Instead of saying I hope, say, *I know.* I know is much more confident. I know is definite. I know reflects certainty.

Consider the phrase *I feel*. I feel sounds emotional, uncertain, and wishy-washy. Instead, use *I believe*. I believe has conviction.

Some words can make you sound inauthentic and imprecise. At the interview, you must be your authentic, unique self, so avoid sweeping generalizations. For example, don't use the word *everything*. Think about how this sentence is heard by the interviewer(s): *Everything was a mess and needed to be changed, so I fixed everything.* Not only does this statement fail to convince the interviewer(s) of your problem-solving skills, it also paints with a broad brush and may end up making you appear negative or disgruntled.

This statement is specific and shows initiative: *The testing lab was disorganized, so I rearranged the chemicals and assigned new numbers that simplified the search process.*

Instead of saying, *I might* say, *I will*. I might is tentative. I will is certain. If I tell you that I might run a marathon, will you instantly book a flight so you can cheer for me at the finish line? Of course not. On the other hand, if I tell you that I will run the Marine Corps Marathon in the fall, you can book a flight to Washington right now because you know I will need a pep squad. On the same note, avoid the word *possibly*. Instead, use *definitely*. Definitely is concrete. It's certain. It tells the interviewer that you believe in yourself and in your abilities.

Don't let words that convey uncertainty creep into your dialog. If you find yourself using these words during your interview preparation, change them to absolute terms and practice making your comments using the new words. If during the interview you hear yourself say *I hope* when you planned to say *I know*, just stop. Say, *that's not what I meant to say. I meant to say I know*. That's right. You immediately correct yourself, and then go on with the interview.

Always use words that convey certainty. Using concrete words is one more opportunity to convince the interviewer(s). Think about an attorney in a courtroom. A lawyer giving closing remarks would never say, *I think*, *I hope*, or *possibly*. To convince a jury, the lawyer must use definitive, concrete words. You do the same to convince the interviewer(s).

~ 3 ~

ANSWERING CRITICAL QUESTIONS

There are four questions for which you must have excellent answers. For each, merely having the right answer is not good enough. You must have an exceptional answer!

1. Can you tell me a little bit about yourself?
2. Why should I hire you?
3. Why do you want this job?
4. Do you have anything else you would like to add?

Let's dive in and design excellent answers.

Tell Me about Yourself: The Opening Statement

The interview often opens with the question: Will you please tell me a little bit about yourself? You may also hear *Tell me about your background* or *tell me about your qualifications for this job*. Let's discuss how to answer. Instead of thinking about a simple answer, think of *tell me about yourself* as a simple sounding question that asks for your critical opening statement.

Photo by August de Richelieu from Pexels

The opening statement is the most important part of the interview. Your opening statement sets the tone for the entire meeting. Your opening statement will determine if the interviewer(s) believe that you are excited about the job, if they think you are an engaging person, and if you are a viable candidate, a perception that will color how they hear your responses to subsequent questions. A well-written, well-rehearsed opening statement will absolutely separate you from the other candidates.

First, let's look at some common mistakes. If you know what to avoid, you'll be better prepared to create a winning opening statement. Some candidates talk too long, and some don't spend enough time on this question. Some candidates fail to express gratitude. They don't connect their experiences with the job requirements. They rehash their resume, which the interviewer(s) have already read.

Clearly, you can remember to express gratitude and to speak for an appropriate amount of time, but how do you avoid giving a verbal resume summary? That's why you are reading this book.

Here's how to prepare an opening statement that sets the right tone.

Keep your answer between 90 seconds and two minutes. Research tells us that after two minutes, interviewers get restless and will cut you off, politely of course. You don't want to be cut off, so end your opening statement around the two-minute mark. However, don't be too short. The remainder of the interview is influenced by this one statement. Since you have two minutes, use that time!

To use this critical time effectively, design your opening

statement like an old-fashioned letter. Your statement will have three parts: the greeting, the body, and the complimentary close.

Oddly, you begin your opening statement by saying thank you. Saying thank you may seem like a small gesture, but it's powerful. Expressing gratitude is proper etiquette and an expected part of the interview protocol. These two words are essential—seasoned interviewers will notice if they are missing.

Ideally, include thank you in both the greeting and the complimentary close. This practice guards against nerves. If your nerves cause you to omit a thank you at the beginning of your opening statement, you have another chance at the end.

Forgetting to say thank you is a huge mistake. Plan to include thank you in your greeting and your closing so that you'll remember to say it at least once. If you say it twice, it's okay.

Here's an example. First, you greet the interviewer(s). You'll say something like, *it's a pleasure to meet you, (use their names). I'm looking forward to this interview. Thank you very much for this opportunity.*

The body of the opening statement divides into three categories: your past, your present, and the future job. Spend 20 percent of the time discussing your past, 30

Answering Critical Questions

percent discussing your present, and 50 percent talking about the future job.

This formula dedicates most of the available time to how your past and present knowledge and experiences connect to the future job. Dividing your time this way helps you convey how confident you are that you can perform the job successfully.

You made it to the interview because somebody already decided that you're qualified. Therefore, don't spend too much time convincing the interviewer(s) that you're qualified. Instead, focus on your work experiences, past responsibilities, and current responsibilities. Order them chronologically. Start way back (but no further back than ten years) and work up to the present, but don't write your memoir! The only reason to go back further than 10 years is if you are interviewing for a job that you did more than 10 years ago but have not done since.

Only speak about things that are relevant to the future job. If you did something amazing years ago but it's not related to this job, don't talk about it. Use the opening statement to connect the dots for the interviewer(s). Which past events prepared you for this job? Don't get in the weeds. Only connect the dots with your significant contributions.

Remember, 50 percent of your time will be used to

address the future. As you do this, focus on intention and motivation. Speak to why you want the job and how you know that you will perform it well.

Interviewers want to separate those who see the opportunity as just a job from those that find this opportunity truly exciting. Make sure they understand exactly why you want the job. Try this approach: *I'm interested in this job because it will allow me to use my writing skills in a meaningful way.* Follow this statement up with how your experiences fit the job, how your personality fits the team, and how your skills, abilities, and core values fit the company culture. Your research will help prepare this answer.

Throughout your opening statement, you're connecting the dots, so the interviewer(s) are convinced that you are a good match. Make sure to mention the proactive activities you took to prepare for this job. For example, maybe a couple of years ago, you examined your career and decided that it was time to pursue the next step. You knew that you would eventually leave your current job and seek another. As you researched, you learned that this type of position fit your goal, but you also saw that you had some skill gaps. Maybe you took some proactive steps. Maybe you got certified in a particular software application. Maybe you went to graduate school. Did you take on additional duties to improve your qualification? Mention how you used the past three years to prepare yourself for this job.

You might say something like this: *You know, three years ago, I looked at my career, and decided that it was time to take the next step. I desired something that fit my goal of career growth. That is why I'm interviewing today; this job is that job! I prepared over the last three years by doing x, y, and z to make sure that I was ready when I was given this opportunity.*

Be specific when mentioning what you did. The final part of the opening statement will explain how you separate yourself from your competition. You'll present how you are different and offer unique knowledge and experiences to the company.

Once you've reached the end of your opening statement, you must indicate that you're ready to move on to the rest of the interview. This is the complimentary close, and it's important because they asked the open-ended question. For example, you might say, *That's a little bit about me. Thank you. I know you have additional questions.*

Giving your opening statement a definitive ending, allows you to insert another thank you. Also, when you indicated that you are finished, you convey confidence that you're ready to move on with the interview. You make it clear that you're not there to ramble and take up the interviewer(s)' time. Try this phrase: *Thank you, I know you have additional questions; I'm ready.*

Remember to get to the complimentary close in under two minutes. You don't want to be stopped because you have gone too long and strayed from the intent of the question.

Sample Opening Statement

Good morning, it's a pleasure to meet all of you. I'm excited about this position and appreciate the opportunity to interview with HDI, thank you. To highlight some experiences that make me a good fit for this job . . . (remember to make the connections). What I bring to your team is . . . Several things I've done to specifically prepare myself to be successful in this job are . . . I see myself being unique in the following way(s) . . . That's a little bit about me. I know you have more questions, and I'm ready. Thank you again.

Design your answer this way, and it will sound excellent—there's no doubt about it. You have a greeting, a body that includes the past, the present, and the future, and a complimentary close. The statement will be easy to remember because you prepared the body

Answering Critical Questions

chronologically.

Let's take it to the next level. A few people already design their answers using this format, but you want to stand out from everyone—even those few. Have you ever heard of the delivery rule? The delivery rule is a simple way to get in front of the pack.

The delivery rule says that you always deliver the most important part of your answer first. So, let's mix it up a little. Try taking some of your future content and speaking about it before you discuss the past. Restructure the design only slightly. You'll have a greeting, a little bit of the future, the body (past, present, and more future), and finally the complimentary close.

Sample Opening Statement Using the Delivery Rule

Good morning, it's a pleasure to meet all of you. I'm excited about this position and appreciate the opportunity to interview with HDI, thank you. I want this job, and I'd like to tell you specifically why I am excited about it . . . (future).

Let me take you back to where I started my career and where I gained the experiences that give me the ideal background to be successful in this job . . . (remember to make the connections). What I bring to your team is . . . Several things I've done to specifically prepare myself to be successful in this job are . . .

I see myself being unique in the following way(s) . . . That's a little bit about me. I know you have additional questions, and I'm ready. Thank you again.

It's a subtle but powerful change. I guarantee you this opening statement will separate you from your competition, and that's what you want.

Twenty-Second Opening

Now that you've learned how to design a memorable opening statement, let's look at how to prepare for less traditional interview scenarios. What happens if instead of opening with *tell me about yourself*, the interviewer(s) open with, *can you give an example of a time you had a conflict at work*?

You think, W*ait! I'm supposed to give my opening statement first; this question is usually asked later in the interview.* What should you do?

Remember, not all interviewer(s) design their interviews the same way, and the interview flow can go in many directions. That's why you'll prepare a 20-second opening statement.

When you get blindsided by an atypical opening question like, *give an example of a time you had a conflict at work*, I suggest you take control without seeming rude.

Say something like this: *I'd be happy to tell you about such a time, but before I begin, I'd like to say thank you for this interview. I've been looking forward to it, and I'm excited to be here. If given the opportunity, I am confident that I will be successful. To answer your first question . . .*

All you did was extract critical sentences from your opening statement and reduce the original down to 20-seconds. You included a thank you, how excited you are to be there, and why you believe you will be successful in the job. These are all vital components of your opening statement, and you were still able to deliver them. Bravo!

Why Should I Hire You?

Why should I hire you? When you hear this question, you'll know that what interviewer(s) really want is help making their decision. Make it easy for them. *Why should I hire*

Photo by Pixabay from Pexels

you begs you to separate yourself from your competition. This is your chance to speak openly and creatively about the value you will bring to the company. Prepare your answer in advance so you don't lose this opportunity!

Why should I hire you gives you space to talk about your uniqueness—the preferred qualifications you have that match the job profile. Remember, you are unique. Your lived experience is only yours. No one else brings what you bring to the table. Don't be bashful! This is the time to sell yourself, your skills, and your experiences that make you the right fit for this job. When answering this question, make sure to say that you are confident of your success!

When you answer *why should I hire you*, remember the power phrases, and use them.

This may sound contradictory, but selling yourself is not about communicating how wonderful you are. Instead, you must convince the interviewer(s) that they will benefit from hiring you. There is a difference!

For example, if you are interviewing internally and your company spent a great deal of time and money training you for a position, you can use that sell yourself. You can say, *The Company spent a lot of time and money training me to be a leader. Give me the opportunity to repay that investment and show them that was money*

Answering Critical Questions

well spent.

Think about basic marketing. Advertisers don't try to sell a product, per se. They sell the idea that your life is missing something. Once they convince you that your life is incomplete, then they tell you how their product will make you feel whole. Your sales job is no different. You are the product that will make work more efficient, and perhaps more lucrative, for the company. Now go sell yourself.

Why Do You Want This Job?

This question asks about your motivation. Interviewers want to know if this is a job that excites you. Does the work interest you? Is it work that you know you can do because you've done it before? They're also listening for those candidates who can do the job but aren't really interested in it. Is it just a job that will pay the bills?

If you want to be impactful, come to the interview excited! The candidate who is not particularly excited has very little energy when answering the question, *why do you want this job?* The answers just lie there—they're flat;

they have no oomph and no vitality. These low-energy candidates don't talk about the satisfaction they receive from serving. They don't mention how much they appreciate being able to contribute. They never speak about physical, mental, or emotional satisfaction.

On the other hand, someone who is excited about the job shows it. Trust me, the company wants committed employees, not employees who are moderately disengaged before they even begin.

Respond to this question with enthusiasm. Interviewer(s) need to hear enthusiasm in your voice, see enthusiasm in your eyes, and catch enthusiasm from your body language. Everything about you should say, *I want this job!*

Be specific about the reasons you want the job. Say something like this: *I want this job. Let me tell you exactly what about this job excites me. I've been waiting for this kind of opportunity. It's exactly the work I want to do.* Be extremely specific about it. Talk about the satisfaction you feel when you can contribute at this level. Talk about how your ability to mentor brings you a sense of purpose. Talk about everything that makes you feel good about this opportunity. Say something like, *this is a place where I believe I'm going to be able to give back to the company the most.* Follow up on this opener by talking about exactly why that is.

Imagine how interviewers feel about a candidate who answers with something like this: *Out of all the research that I did, learning about the company, the job, and the culture, this position is the one that is most attractive to me. This position is a perfect match for my background, what I'm interested in doing and where I believe I can contribute the most to the company. I'm interested in what you have to offer and am looking forward to hearing more.*

Show confidence that you will be successful. Use power phrases. Sell yourself mightily in this answer.

Do You Have Anything You'd Like to Add?

The Closing Statement

Your closing statement is the second most crucial response in the interview. Think about attorneys in a courtroom. How do they prepare their opening and closing statements? Attorneys know that the opening and closing statements have won many trials, so they prepare these statements extremely well. In the same way, your closing statement is the last thing you say before you leave the room. That means it's the last thing you say before the interviewer(s) look at their notes to evaluate you. Do they want to hire you or not? You've worked hard on your interview preparation. Don't make the mistake of thinking that your closing statement will take care of itself!

Do you realize that many candidates decline when asked if they have anything they want to add? Imagine you hired a lawyer to represent you. What would you do if, when presented with the opportunity to deliver a closing statement, your lawyer said, *No, I don't have anything else*? I hope you would fire them.

Since the closing statement is so critical, let's design one that will be positively unforgettable.

In terms of your delivery, I want you to take your time. Speak slowly and clearly so that everyone on the panel hears every word. As if you are on stage, when you complete a sentence, pause before you give the next sentence. Make sure you know your closing statement so well you can deliver it without referring to your notes. The best way to appear confident is to lock in, make great eye contact, use an assertive tone, and end strong. Looking at your notes undermines this approach.

In your closing statement, personalize the goodbye, so

Answering Critical Questions

that it's not too long. Lengthy good-byes are just awkward. Keep your closing statement between 45 and 60 seconds. Although this statement is fairly brief, it should be strong.

As with the opening statement, begin and end with a thank you and use powerful phrases.

You may even wish to include some reiterated statements. For an extra punch and to show that you've been listening, mention how you can solve the problems created by the vacancy.

The thank you at the beginning sounds something like this: *I'd just like to thank you once again for the opportunity to interview.* When you reach the end of your closing statement, your thank you will be more personable. By now, you understand the mood of the interview. You know if it's formal, informal, or maybe even casual. Let's look at how to say thank you to match the environment.

Formal—*Thank you. It would be my pleasure to be part of your team.*

Informal—*Thank you. It's been a pleasure meeting you.*

Informal—*Thank you for your time today. I look forward to hearing from you.*

Casual—*Thank you. This was a fabulous opportunity.*

I enjoyed it.

Earlier we said you'd use two thank-yous and power phrases. Power phrases sound like this, *I've been preparing to do this job. I'm confident that I'll be successful. I take great pride in my work ethic and all the ways I can add value to the team.* Use power phrases at the end of your closing statement.

Also, I mentioned the reiterated statements. There might be one or two things that you said earlier in the interview that you want them to hear one more time, right before you walk out the door. Go ahead and point out that you are reiterating something you already said. This tells the interviewer(s) that you think it's critical for them to understand. Just begin with something like, *as I mentioned earlier . . .*

You've been waiting for the right moment to tell them you want the job. This is it. Try using a statement like this: *I listened to what you had to say about the job, and I've picked up on your priorities through the questions that you asked. I know for sure now that this is the right job for me. I want this job.*

Finally, if you picked up on an issue that you can solve, make sure they know that you can make their problems go away. Not only do you show how you can make their work more efficient, but you also show them that it's not all about you. You have been listening to them and wish to help. You may say something like this, *I heard you say that sales in the southwest region have not been what you had hoped they would be. You said that the previous account manager did a great job of bringing your product and brand recognition to the region, but now you need someone who can develop it more fully. I already have some ideas. I know I can solve this problem because previously, I . . .*

Now let's put it all together and see how our closing statement looks.

> Since the closing statement is so critical...
> ... design one that will be *positively unforgettable.*

I want to thank you again for this interview. It's been a pleasure meeting you. I'm certain this is the right job for me at this point in my career. It's exactly what I want to do, what I do well, and where I believe I can help the company the most. For example, I heard you say that record-keeping is cumbersome. I know I can help with this issue because I am very interested in PowerBI, and I know it can simplify not only record-keeping but data analytics as well. There's no doubt in my mind that I can add value to the team if given the chance. As I mentioned at the beginning, I've already been successful using the skills required for this job, and my background is a perfect match for its demands. I'm certain if, given the opportunity, I will meet or exceed your expectations, and I ask that you give me the chance to prove it. Thank you again for this interview. I look forward to becoming a part of your team."

That's how you give an excellent closing statement.

Twenty-Second Closing

Like the 20-second opening statement, I want you to create a 20-second closing. You must be prepared in case the interviewer(s) don't toss you the standard final question, *do you have anything else you would like to say?* They may say something quite formal, such as *We completed our questions. Thanks for coming in.* Don't stand up and leave! You still need to deliver your closing statement, however abbreviated.

To prepare, extract critical sentences from your closing statement and create a 20-second closing statement.

Include a thank-you, how excited you are about the job, and why you believe you will be successful. These are vital components of your closing statement, and you will deliver them.

Consider this 20-second closing statement: *Before I go, I want to say thank you again for this opportunity. It was a real pleasure, and I'm certain this is the right job for me at this point in my career. I know I'd be successful if given the opportunity.* On this confident note, turn and leave.

By using the 20-second closing statement, even if you are cheated out of your grand finale, you are still able to say the essential things and end the interview on your terms.

Behavioral Answers

The answers to behavioral questions will be the most natural answers for you. Behavioral questions are open-ended questions that give you the latitude to discuss things you have already accomplished and how you would accomplish something challenging in the future. These questions ask you to access your memory and tell your story. You will have many behavioral questions in your job search. Don't be afraid of them. The questions come in two forms: a hypothetical question and an example question. Let's review each separately.

A hypothetical question typically asks, *what would you do if* . . . Both the question's hypothetical situation and your answer are worded in the future tense. Hypothetical questions invite weak responses because they are questions about something that hasn't happened yet.

An example question typically asks, *can you give me an example of a time when you* . . . Both the question and the answer are past tense. Unlike hypothetical questions, example questions invite strong answers because you can point to something that you did. The best answer that you can give conveys a message through your story. The interviewer learns that you've been there, done that successfully, many times. Interviewers want to hear that message because the best predictor of your future success is what you accomplished in the past.

I'm suggesting that you use example answers as much as possible. Obviously, an example question invites an example answer. But what if they give you that darned hypothetical question? Take a moment and search your memory. Find a time when something similar to the hypothetical happened to you. Once you have this memory, you provide an example answer just as if it were an example question.

For example, you may hear, *what would you do if . . .* Think about it and reply, *well, that happened to me. Let me tell you what I did.* As much as possible, answer hypothetical questions with example answers because example answers have something that a hypothetical answer can never have: results. Interviewers want to hear concrete information. They want results.

> *The best predictor of your future success is what you accomplished in the past.*

Behavioral questions can be troubling because candidates often feel that interviewers are looking for an exact answer. But that is not true. You can approach behavioral questions in several ways. Let's think through a question about a time you had a conflict with a teammate and how the situation resolved.

Your first option is to give them an exact example. You

tell them about a time you had a conflict with a teammate and how you resolved it to keep the team cohesive. An answer like this exactly matches their question. But what if you can't think of a single example of such a situation?

If you don't have an exact example, option two is to answer with a similar example from work. Perhaps you had a conflict with a supervisor, a customer, or someone on a team that works closely with yours. This similar example is still a strong answer because the question is not about the person with whom you had the conflict. The question is about how well you resolved it. But what if you don't have a similar example from work?

If you don't have a similar example from work, you can discuss a similar example outside of work. You explain that you don't have a case of a conflict with someone at work, but you disagreed with your neighbor once. Discuss that experience. Remember, the question is really about how well you resolve conflict, not about the person you disagreed with. But what if you are averse to conflict and can't think of any example at all?

If you still don't have an answer, you can design a hypothetical reply. Remember, hypothetical answers are inherently weak because they haven't happened yet, but you can strengthen your response.

When you design a hypothetical answer, think about

the values that dictate your actions. In other words, when you think about resolving conflict, what is important? You may believe the best way to resolve conflict is to work towards a win-win solution. You may believe that respecting each other despite disagreements is critical. Maybe really listening, even when it's complicated, is what matters to you. Your hypothetical answer should reflect your values. Make sure the interviewer sees the connection between your values and how you would handle the situation. So, you might say, *I don't have a specific example of a conflict with someone, but when I think about resolving conflict, the most important thing is working toward a win-win solution. Based on that, I would ...*

One last tip: More is not better. Deliver only one example per question. When you offer two examples to a question, it weakens your overall answer because it suggests that you do not believe your first example was good enough.

Take the time to create and provide thoughtful responses to behavioral questions.

The STAR Method

The STAR method is a step-by-step approach to design answers to behavioral questions. The acronym STAR stands for situation, task, action, and result. The situation is the experience or hypothetical question, the task is the challenge in the question, the action is the steps required to complete the task, and the result is the outcome. This acronym is interesting because components begin with the least important (situation) and grow to the most important (result).

When answering a behavioral question, spend only a small amount of time on the situation and the task. Focus on what is important: action and result.

Answering Critical Questions

First, ensure your situation matches the question and is appropriate for the interview. Think of a situation that had a positive outcome, never a negative one. Sufficiently but succinctly review the situation, including only the information needed for the interviewer(s) to understand the circumstances.

The task is related to both the situation and the action, so make sure the task (the challenge) is associated with the situation and can be remedied through logical action steps. Again, only briefly describe the task. Now you can dive into the meaty part of your answer.

The action is exactly what it says. This is your opportunity to review the steps you took to address the task (the challenge). Your discussion will sound like this: *First, I did this. After that was successful, I...* Keep going until the task (the challenge) is resolved.

In the situation and task part of your answer, you wanted to be succinct. Not now. In the action portion of your answer, take time to explain why your actions made sense—maybe even why they were innovative. You were involved in the situation, but the interviewer(s) are new to the experience. Make your memory an engaging trip and bring the interviewer(s) along with you. Now that everyone is involved in the experience, you can wow them with the results.

When you arrive at the result, the most critical part of the answer, end with a positive outcome. Include in your outcome what you learned from the situation. Interviewer(s) like to hear about learning experiences because they show your willingness to see opportunities instead of problems. For extra zing, include how both you and the company benefited. To summarize, you explain the positive result, identify what you learned, and reveal how both you and the company benefited.

Unfortunately, the STAR answer ends with the result, which contradicts the delivery rule that we discussed when building an opening statement. Remember, the delivery rule states that you always deliver the most important part of your answer first. How do you cope with having your most important information last? What if the interviewers have a short attention span? What if you are the final candidate of the day, and they are tired? Let's think about how we might apply the delivery rule to the STAR system.

After you write your answer using STAR, take a bit of your result—just enough to create curiosity—and position it before the situation. This will be about 1/3 of your result text. In media, they call this a *teaser*. Consider the conflict-with-a-teammate question. Your result teaser might sound like this: *Yes, I can tell you about a time when I had a conflict with a teammate. I'm very glad that the conflict occurred because this person and I are now friends. Now, we're learning from each other instead of having a conflict. Let me tell you about it.* You teased the result, and now your listeners are curious. The remainder of your answer will follow the STAR method.

While the STAR method and the result teaser generate fantastic answers, you can still take your answer to the next level! I believe that interviews are much more about what *you* want to tell interviewers than what interviewers want to know. That's where commentaries come into play.

When you walk into the interview with prepared answers, you can use commentaries. A commentary is a statement that prefaces your answer. Offer a commentary to highlight a positive character trait or job qualification. Ask yourself, what can I say about conflict that puts me in a good light? The commentary you create helps establish a positive perception with the interviewer(s). All you do is take a little bit of your commentary and put it before the situation. After the commentary, you'll share a bit of the result, and then you'll follow STAR to the end of your answer.

Now you have six steps to answer the question, *can you tell me of a time you had a conflict with a teammate?* You might respond as follows:

Commentary: *I don't have much conflict. I decided a long time ago before I attempt to get people to understand me; I strive to understand them. I listen and paraphrase. Often this translates into a respectful discussion of differing viewpoints and avoids conflict.*

Result Teaser: *I can, however, remember a specific misunderstanding. I'm glad it happened because this person and I are friends now. Let me tell you about it.*

Situation: *We were working on a project, and I sent her an email. She thought my tone in the email was demeaning, and she got upset. She sent me an email telling me so, but I didn't understand her point because using a demeaning tone was not my intention. We were both frustrated.*

Task: *I knew that we needed to clear up the confusion and get on the same page before things escalated.*

Action: *I suggested we meet in person and discuss our perspectives. After we both listened to each other, we identified the problem. We decided that our project is so technical it would be better if we got together twice a week to discuss things in person rather than by email because email invites misinterpretation.*

Result: *Doing this allows us to explain the technical concepts in detail versus in email. The added benefit is the opportunity to invite teammates who can add to our discussion. Now, the entire team is getting to know each other better and working well together.*

Behavioral Categories and Trigger Words

Behavioral questions help interviewers understand your skills, abilities, and personality by learning how you handle typical work situations. To be prepared for almost any behavioral question, you need to understand behavioral categories. Behavioral categories are the behaviors that the company selected as necessary to job success. You can find these on the position description. The interviewer(s) take the job requirements from the position description and develop behavioral questions using these categories.

Behavioral categories often include:
- Adaptability
- Communication
- Conflict resolution
- Decision making
- Developing people

- Diversity
- Taking initiative
- Motivating others

This is not an exhaustive list of behavioral categories. You can find many more on the Internet. Use the position description to create your list of categories. You may have 15 – 20. Next, take a best guess at which of these you think the interviewer(s) may have selected. Which 5 – 10 categories seem like the most important.

Once you have the categories, think of potential questions and design an answer to each. For example, if the job requirement is a leadership role, a category might be developing people. Interviewer(s) might say, *give me an example of how you make sure that your employees continually develop their skills*. Another development question could be, *tell me what you have done to retain your employees*. Design an answer for both questions.

For the most relevant categories, design two answers. For the remaining categories, create only one answer. You could theoretically come up with 15 – 30 example questions and answers. That's a lot to remember, but I have a trick: trigger words.

Once you have all your answers designed and finalized, think of a word or phrase that will remind you of your answer. Write this word or phrase next to the behavioral category. These are your trigger words. Rely on them.

Realistically, 15 – 30 trigger words still take up a lot of memory space. Let's reduce the number by doubling-up. Use the same example or the same story for two different categories. To prevent overlap (and the embarrassing situation of having the same answer to two questions), be strategic. Use an example for one category that is highly likely to produce a question and one category that is less likely to produce a question.

When you conduct this time-consuming exercise on behavioral categories, you will reap two significant rewards. First, you will answer the interview questions articulately, clearly, and confidently. Second, like boot camp, the discipline of this process will mentally prepare you to be on top of your game, regardless of what questions are asked.

The Weakness Questions: Turning

Weaknesses into Strengths

Research suggests that up to 75 percent of interview decisions not to hire a candidate result from weakness questions. You can hope that the interviewer doesn't ask you a weakness question, but they probably will. Like all other questions, you must prepare for them. Following are some typical weakness questions, but you'll find many more with a quick Google search:

• What are some of your most obvious weaknesses?

• What areas would you like to develop the most, and why?

• What is your biggest shortcoming related to your performance?

• Tell me about a situation where you struggled at work and how you are handling it now.

• Tell me of a time when your efforts to influence a situation were ineffective. As with all types of interview answers, you can design great answers to weakness questions using some general guidelines.

1. <u>Do not use words that convey negativity</u>, such as weakness, shortcoming, or struggle. Because negative words can pop up unexpectedly, you must practice avoiding them. They often show up when you innocently repeat the question as part of your answer. For example, the interviewer says, *tell me one of your weaknesses*. And you say, *one of my weaknesses is* . . . Oh my gosh, what did you say!

First, you used the word *weakness*. Don't do that! *Weakness* is negative. Second, you said, *one of* my weaknesses. Now, you've said that you have more than one! Do not do this!

Instead, I want you to choose positive wording to set-up your response. Rather than saying, *one of my weaknesses is*, try this: *My manager suggested that I could be better if I would*... See, that sounds much better. Or maybe, *someone once shared with me that I could be a top performer in my field if I would*... These are positive, not negative responses.

2. <u>Never volunteer a weakness</u>. It is incredible to me that some candidates volunteer their shortcomings without being asked. I'll use the question I've used throughout this course: *Can you give me an example of a time you had a conflict with a teammate?* The candidate answers, *Hm. Let me think for a moment. I've probably had more conflict than most people.* Why would they do that? Look again at my suggested responses above for guideline number one. Even when explicitly asked for a weakness, you won't give one. You certainly don't want to offer one without being asked!

3. <u>Make sure that any weakness you mention is not critical to the position</u>. This is really important! I just

don't understand why some candidates make this mistake. If you are interviewing for a communications job and the interviewer asks you to share a weakness, don't say that your manager told you that you needed to improve your writing skills.

When I was interviewing a candidate for a leadership position and asked about his greatest weakness, he replied, "My manager told me that I don't motivate and delegate." No way! Motivating and delegating are critical skills for a leader. Why did he choose that example?

Sometimes, candidates feel that they can recover from a lousy answer by saying something like, *this was a weakness, but I improved.* No such luck. The interviewer(s) formed their impressions as soon as the candidate mentioned needing improvement on a skill that was critical to the position.

As you keep these three guidelines in mind, let's design answers to weakness questions, using nine design strategies.

Weakness Question Strategy #1

Mention the necessary improvement as pointed out by your manager, and then immediately expound on what you're doing to work on it. Finally, mention the progress that you have made. Consider this example: *My manager suggested that I should improve the lines of communication with my employees. I took this observation seriously and worked on it by . . . (explain the steps you chose). After three months, I can tell I've made significant progress because . . . (be specific).*

To summarize, strategy #1 uses the three-part method: the deficiency, your action, and your progress.

Weakness Question Strategy #2

This strategy is the same as strategy #1, but with one change. Instead of your manager pointing out your deficiency, you point it out to yourself. Strategy #2 is a proactive answer. You don't wait for someone to notice an area in which you need to improve. Instead, you recognized that you could benefit from improving in a specific area. Complete that answer by sharing what you're doing to work on it and the improvement you have made. This answer is very safe since nobody else mentioned you needed improvement. It's your proactive measures that resulted in your improvement.

Weakness Question Strategy #3

Overshadow the weakness with a strength. Downplay the criticism by including an impressive strength or advantage that outweighs the weakness. The point is that the hiring manager may tolerate the weakness and hire you because of the strength.

Let's design the answer using this strategy. Your weakness is that you appear disorganized because you have a messy office. Your strength is that you are incredibly productive. Mention that you accomplish a tremendous amount of work, but on occasion, you place things on your desk in random places. Tidying time would slow down your work output, and the state of your desk has never hindered your ability to do your job. It's just a perception issue. The hiring manager might decide she can tolerate a messy office to have a highly productive employee.

Can you see how answering a question in this way requires preparation? Always prepare for the weakness questions in advance.

Weakness Question Strategy #4

Turn a weakness into a strength. Explain that as you worked on your weakness, you saw so much value in improvement that you didn't stop until you developed the weakness into a strength. For instance, you knew that you could improve your computer skills. So, you started taking computer classes and found that you enjoyed them immensely. You could have stopped and been proficient at your job, but you continued with additional classes. Now, you're the most computer savvy person in the department.

Your computer proficiency evolved from a developmental need to one of your most reliable skills.

Weakness Question Strategy #5

Recognize that some weaknesses are like an overuse sports injury. They develop due to the overuse of a strength. Share that you are learning to use your strength to its utmost while not overusing it, which could make it a weakness. You might say something like this: *I have tremendous analytical troubleshooting skills. If I'm not careful, I can spend too much time troubleshooting and analyzing an issue, get bogged down, and ultimately, get less accomplished. I balance my efforts by identifying how much analysis is required to solve the problem before I start the project. When I get to that point, I stop my review and implement my results. In this way, I use my strength of analysis and avoid a slow-down in my productivity.*

Weakness Question Strategy #6

Address an area of improvement that would benefit your current job but would not impact the future position. As always, include steps you are taking to improve. This answer is safe because the weakness is not relevant to the job for which you are interviewing.

Weakness Question Strategy #7

Share that a developmental need exists only because the skill was just recently required. Since the skill is a new requirement at your current job, a reasonable person would expect it will take some time to develop. An excellent example is when your job responsibilities change. You have new job functions that you have not performed before. To complete the responsibility successfully, you need to develop the new skill. It's understandable if some development is still needed.

Weakness Question Strategy #8

Reveal a strength that is necessary to excel at your job. Even though it is one of your strengths, you seek to continuously improve it. As always, share exactly what you are doing to get even better in this area. For example, *as a trainer, one of my strengths is listening to the participants who take my courses so I can identify the best way to assist them. While this is one of my strengths, it is essential to my job. I am always looking for ways to improve. What I'm doing now is . . .* Now, explain the steps you're taking to improve your listening.

Weakness Question Strategy #9

Share only one weakness or area needing development.

Answering Critical Questions

If the interviewer(s) ask you to identify two weaknesses, identify only one and stop. Only offer a second if the interviewer(s) call your bluff and ask you for a second one. Never provide a laundry list of areas needing improvement.

I suggest you prepare a minimum of two to three weakness answers for your interview. Then select the one that best fits their question, when asked.

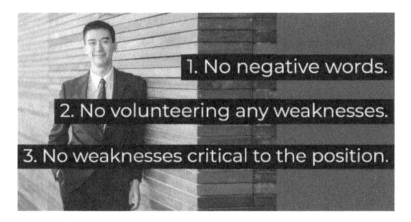

~ 4 ~

PERFECTING YOUR ANSWERS

Great answers don't just happen. Yes, sometimes a candidate can answer one or two questions fairly well without preparation, but a candidate's overall preparedness is very obvious to the interviewer(s). If you focus and take the time to design winning answers, you will easily separate yourself from the crowd! Let's talk about how to dig in and find the gems that will make the interviewer(s) want to hire you as soon as possible. We'll get those answers darned near perfect!

Designing Great Answers

As you walk into the interview, I don't want you to have good answers, I want you to have GREAT answers. You'll have great answers when you follow this six-step process.

The first step is to brainstorm everything that you may want to include in your answer. Since everyone needs an opening statement, let's practice with this. You may recall that the opening statement follows the *tell-me-about-yourself* question. I know this exercise may sound a bit like a review, but hang with me.

Step 1

Begin brainstorming the information you want to

Photo by Per Lööv on Unsplash

include in your opening statement. Remember, brainstorming is an uninhibited exercise. Don't edit yourself. Get everything on paper, and you can refine it later. Often, the most creative solutions are the ones that appear after you think you've exhausted all your answers.

Here are ideas to get you started. You'll want to introduce yourself. You'll thank the interviewer(s) for the interview. You'll talk a little bit about your qualifications, experience, and skill set. You'll make sure the interviewer(s) know that you want the job, why you want the job, and how you fit the company culture. Write down all this information.

Step 2

After exhausting all your ideas, convert those words and phrases into individual sentences. For example, you wrote down, *thank the interviewer.* This thought becomes, *I'd first like to thank you for the opportunity to interview.* You wrote *I want the job* and *reasons why I want the job.* These thoughts become, *I'd like you to know that I want this job because I've done this work successfully throughout my career and am very passionate about it.*

Step 3

Take the individual sentences and put them in a logical order so that they flow smoothly together.

The first sentence—I want to thank you for the interview.

Next—I'm excited to be here, and I want this job.

Next—I've done this kind of work successfully my entire career, and I'm passionate about it.

Next—I've acquired the skills necessary to meet the job (name them).

Last—The positions I've held previously have prepared me to do this job well (name them).

Step 4

Step four is the magical step. Your thoughts, developed into sentences, are now sequenced for smooth delivery. This is where things begin to come together. But don't stop here. You don't really know if they flow together smoothly until you hear them audibly. Read the sentences aloud and audio-record them. Don't use a camera. Listen to your recorded answer and make any necessary edits.

You may discover that your first edit will be lengthening or clarifying the existing content. As you played your recorded answer, there was a sentence that sounded good when you wrote it, but not so good when you heard it. Maybe it wasn't clear. Adding a few clarifying words might make it more easily understandable.

Another place to look for edits is in long sentences. Maybe you sound a little long-winded or pompous because you used some unnecessary words or jargon. So, find ways to simplify your content.

A third place to edit may be removing content. For example, there may be one or two sentences that seemed relevant when you wrote them but sounded out of place when you heard them. Take them out.

Finally, you may find that you need some new content. You may need to repeat the brainstorming exercise or look at items that you thought were unimportant. This is a great place for you to include information that you didn't think about in step one.

Step 5

Step 5 repeats steps 3 and 4 with purpose. Now that you've mixed things up a bit—adding content here and removing and changing content over there—your answer may not flow smoothly anymore. It may need to be re-sequenced or re-edited. If you want to take it to the next level, try pasting your answer into an online text-to-speech (TTS) generator. Hearing your answer in another voice may reveal more clearly the areas that need some work.

Repeat steps three and four as many times as necessary. Re-sequence the answer, read it, record it, play it back, and edit. Do it again and again. Repeat this cycle until you hear your answer and know with conviction that it's perfect.

Step 6

Finally, you must sufficiently practice the answer, so that when the time comes, you provide the answer smoothly and confidently. There is no substitute for practice.

Answering without Sounding Scripted

When practicing your answers, you may become concerned that your answers sound scripted, over-rehearsed, or even robotic. The difference in how your answer sounds depends upon how much you have practiced. Let's imagine your practice on a spectrum ranging from not practicing at all to practicing well.

On the very low end of the spectrum, you're just winging it. It will sound like you walked in and hoped for the best.

Next, consider what happens with minimal preparation. This is where you know you didn't practice sufficiently. Things got in the way. Life happened. Unfortunately, minimal preparation leads to answers that sound like minimal preparation.

Further across the spectrum, you've prepared a little bit more. Now your answer sounds pretty good, but not polished.

Just beyond *pretty good, but not polished*, you reach the point where you've practiced just enough to sound scripted. As you practice your answer two or three times in a row, you notice that it sounds unnatural and robotic. It is here that you may convince yourself to stop short. Don't do this!

I really believe that you must reach the point of sounding scripted before you can move towards conversational answers. Once you get past that awkward stage, your answer will begin to sound natural. When you've crossed over, you'll know the answer so well that if you forget something, you can start in the middle and easily go back, pick up the beginning, and then end well. Don't be concerned about sounding scripted. Keep practicing, and eventually, the answer will sound smooth and polished.

~ 5 ~

LAST-MINUTE MATTERS

Before you leave home, make sure you are really prepared by taking care of last-minute matters. Of course, you will have prepared your portfolio days in advance, but now you must think about the details.

Photo by Jeffrey Paa Kwesi Opare from Pexels

Have you ever thought about what you eat and drink before an interview? Little things are important. When should you arrive? What should you do after you introduce yourself to the receptionist? We'll cover all of that and more in this important chapter.

The Last Few Hours

Don't let your guard down in the hours before the interview. Some candidates relax at this point, and that may hinder their performance and sabotage their success. Here are some tips and tricks to help you avoid last-minute mistakes.

Tip1

Be prepared. If possible, complete your preparation two or three days before the interview. If the interview is short notice, which does happen, you may not be able to accomplish this. Otherwise, be prepared a few days in advance.

Finishing early is just good planning. You've been studying hard, staying up late, eating poorly, and stressing out to get your answers well-rehearsed. You don't want to carry that exhaustion into the interview. You really do need a day or two to unwind and think positive thoughts about how your dedication, persistence, and preparation are going to pay off. Use this downtime to completely focus totally on the positive. When you walk into the interview, you will shine!

Tip 2

Be early. The night before the interview, go to bed early. Get a good night's rest, wake up refreshed, and arrive early. There is no good excuse for being late—not bad traffic, not a flat tire, not a delayed train. There is almost nothing that's considered an acceptable excuse for late arrival.

Since you can't predict emergencies or even just traffic, it's best to leave early and arrive early. When you get to the location, do whatever works for you to get mentally prepared to do your best. Some people need to ramp up—maybe they listen to energizing music or walk around the building to get their blood flowing. Other people need to calm down—they may listen to relaxing music, read a book, or sit quietly in the car before going inside. Whichever method you choose, make sure it works for you. When you walk into the interview, you'll be ready for peak performance.

Tip 3

Be a picky eater. There are some foods you should avoid. Don't eat mayonnaise or dairy products, such as cheese, milk, or yogurt. These foods can react negatively to your system and create phlegm in your throat. You certainly don't want to clear your throat throughout the whole interview.

Don't chew gum, drink carbonated drinks, or eat spicy food because these can lead to embarrassing sounds while digesting.

Tip 4

Be inoffensive. Don't smoke, and don't eat foods that have strong odors. You don't want to carry those odors with you into the interview. Those odors will linger after you're gone, helping the interviewer(s) remember you, but not in a good way.

Remember this commonsense list of things to do and to avoid in the last few hours! To dismiss them can cost you the job.

Entrance and Exit

Let's really dig into the basics. How should you enter and exit the interview? Arrive early. As you drive onto the company premises, imagine that somebody in the company is watching you. Pretend they are filming you, and they're going to show the video to the hiring manager. Everything you do should show your confidence—getting off the train, getting out of your car, walking into the building.

Never adjust your shirt and tie or put on lipstick in the lobby! Make all adjustments to hair, clothing, and make-up before you arrive. You want to be ready by the time anybody can see you. It's time for your first impression. It's the only one you have, and you want to make it great!

Use this same polished dynamic when exiting. Regardless of how the interview played out, deliver firm handshakes, display confidence, and express gratitude before leaving.

If the interview didn't go the way you had hoped, you may feel discouraged. Don't let this rattle you. It doesn't matter. Don't show disappointment in your body language, facial expression, or handshake. At the beginning of the interview, you were strong and confident. You had a friendly, firm handshake and a big smile. Regardless of whether you feel elated or disappointed, walk out of the room the same way you arrived.

Continue in your polished, confident manner until you have left the company premises. Pretend like the camera is still following you as you're exiting.

Your first impression encompasses all the time from pulling into to driving out of the company parking lot.

Managing your first impression is powerful!

First Impressions

First impressions are critical because first impressions influence final impressions, and final impressions influence hiring decisions.

Let me ask you a question. Have you ever met a new person, and while you didn't know anything about them, you did know that you liked them? Later on, you heard that they're not a very nice person. Upon hearing that, you thought, That doesn't sound right. Or, maybe the opposite scenario happened to you. Maybe you met somebody new, and for some reason, you didn't like them—even though you knew nothing about them. Then later, you heard all kinds of good things about them. You think, Really, that person? How could I have been so wrong? You see, an interesting part of human nature is that people want to be right. We want to trust our first impressions. We want to be able to say to ourselves, I knew it, right from the get-go. Three cognitive biases are at work here: the halo effect, the horns effect, and the confirmation bias.

According to *Psychology Today*, people, "tend to view others holistically, that is, as all good or all bad."[2] This simplistic view comes from the halo effect and the horns effect (think of angels with halos and the devil with horns). When we met that person we liked, we thought that because they were a good conversationalist or even just good looking, they would also be a good person. On the other hand, as soon as we noticed the shabby clothes on the person we didn't like, we decided that they were bad to the core.

When you combine the halo effect and the horns effect with the confirmation bias, we humans are really set up for making some poor decisions. The confirmation bias is our human tendency to prove ourselves right. We ignore any evidence that we are wrong, and we only seek out evidence that proves we are correct. Let's look at how the halo effect, the horns effect, and the confirmation bias work in an interview, and let's further explore how we can take advantage of these all-too-human traits.

Based on these cognitive biases, we know that the interviewer(s) will try to make their first impression match their final impression. It's unavoidable.

---

[2] Causey, Kayla, and Aaron Goetz. "The Halo Effect in Overdrive." *Psychology Today*, Sussex Publishers, 2 July 2009.

It happens like this. Let's say you come into the interview and make a great first impression. During the interview, you're going to do some things really well, and you may do some things not so well. What stands out in the interviewer's mind is whatever they want to see.

If you made an excellent first impression, they'll be on the watch for anything that validates their belief that you are a great person. They want their final impression to match their first impression. They are looking for good things, so that at the end of the interview they will be cognitively comfortable, thinking, *I knew they were going to be good.*

On the flip side, if a candidate makes a negative first impression, the interviewer(s) will be looking for any (and every) mistake they make. Errors will jump out at them. At the end of the interview, they will be cognitively comfortable, thinking, *I knew it! That candidate was terrible.*

So, get in there and make a great first impression. That foundation is key if you want the interviewer(s) to seek out all the great stuff that you do!

Meeting the Greeter

Imagine sitting outside the interview room, trying not to appear nervous while waiting for a mysterious someone to welcome you.

You may expect someone in an administrative role to meet you, but that is not always the case. The person you are waiting on may be the Human Resources representative, the hiring manager, or a future teammate. How exactly should you approach this person?

You approach them as if their role is part of the interview—because it is. Don't let your guard down when touring the facility, either now or later in the interview. A tour is definitely part of the interview. Your guide will be asked about your personality. Are you personable and friendly? Did you ask thoughtful questions? Continue to operate as if the video that started when you arrived is still running as you take a walk around.

Consider asking the greeter some questions. You may ask for some information about the position or the interview. The greeter may even ask if you have any questions before you go into the interview.

Last-Minute Matters

Make it easy on yourself and have greeter questions already written down. You may ask about practical matters, such as is it appropriate to call the interviewer(s) by their first names? Regardless of the answer, note the interviewer(s) names on paper for your reference. You may want to find out if everybody has a copy of your resume. You may think of other relevant questions.

Let's address that question about your resume. It is entirely possible that the interviewer(s) received your resume but didn't bring it to the interview. Remember, not all interviewers are well prepared. Regardless of your greeter's answer, you will have additional copies of your resume with you. Side note: Make sure you also have copies of letters of recommendation, copies of your list of references, and more copies of your resume than you think you'll need. You never know when the hiring manager may add a person or two to the panel at the last minute.

Tell the greeter that you are happy to provide the interviewer(s) your copies. However, neither you nor the greeter should hand them out at the beginning of the interview. Explain to the greeter that you would prefer to hand them out at the end of the interview. Otherwise, your handout will distract the interviewer(s) from giving your answers undivided attention. Providing written information at the last minute almost always invites distraction.

You may hand the interviewer(s) your resumes as you finish your closing statement. Or you may give the copies to the greeter as they walk you to the lobby after the interview. Don't forget to thank the greeter for distributing them to the interviewer(s) for you.

~ 6 ~

DURING THE INTERVIEW

We're finally there, at the interview. Many small details can really set you apart from your competition—things like how you introduce yourself, how you sit, whom you make eye contact with and when, how you position your hands, and more. While this may seem like a lot to think about, most of it comes naturally. Of course, you must practice these nuances to make sure they are so automatic that all you have to think about is your answers.

The Basics

USING NAMES

Following proper etiquette is essential and necessary. Let's address how to meet your interviewer(s), how to introduce yourself properly, and how to address them during the interview.

The proper way to introduce yourself to those whom you are meeting for the first time is to 1) initiate the introduction by giving your first and last name. After that, the interviewer should reciprocate. 2) Repeat the interviewer's first name, and 3) follow with a greeting. Those are the simple steps.

If I were meeting the interviewer, Sasha, I would say, *Hi, my name is Craig DiVizzio*. She would say, *My name is Sasha Miller*. I would say, *Sasha, it's a pleasure to meet you*. Easy as that.

If you have already met someone on the panel, you may be less formal. You may extend your hand and say, *Hi, Bill, good to see you again*. By introducing yourself this way, everybody on the panel will learn whom you already know, and whom you are meeting for the first time. You're not hiding anything. And you're establishing credibility.

If an interviewer doesn't say their name or shake your hand, don't take offense. In a post-pandemic world, etiquette may be changing. Nevertheless, there are different strokes for different folks. Sometimes, this kind of awkwardness could be a test to see how you handle the situation. Regardless, all you have to do is say, *It's a pleasure to meet you*, and move to the next person.

Let's assume that it's a panel interview. After you have greeted everybody, write down the names you learned from the introduction. As soon as you sit down after greeting everybody, it's okay to ask them to repeat their names. Simply say, *Will you be kind enough to give me your name again so I can write it down?* Then, turn to the first person and say, *your name is?* As they say their name, say *thank you* and write their name down in an impromptu (and personal) seating chart. Then, move on to the next interviewer. You now have each name and a seating chart. Good work. Let's make use of it.

What should you do with this valuable information? When Sasha asks a question: *Craig, can you give me an example of a time that you had a conflict with a member of your team?* Before you launch into your answer, say her name in whatever form the greeter told you was appropriate. If first names are appropriate, it will sound something like this: *Sasha, I do have an example.* Then, you answer her behavioral question as we already discussed.

Although this is not difficult, it is critical! If you want to stand out from your competition, get those names down. You will not only establish a great first impression, but you will also personalize your interview answers in a way that makes everyone feel good: by using their names.

EYE CONTACT

You've heard that eye contact is important, but have you given any thought to why? The drive for eye contact is hardwired into the human brain. A study by the National Academy of Sciences

> *Even newborn infants prefer faces who make eye contact.*

revealed that even newborn infants (two to five days old) prefer faces who make eye contact to those that don't.[3]

---

[3] Farroni, Teresa, et al. "Eye Contact Detection in Humans from Birth." *Proceedings of the National Academy of Sciences of the United States of America*, National Academy of Sciences, 9 July 2002.

Eye contact conveys one's inner being—our emotions and intentions. Truly the eyes don't lie. Eye contact is one of the most important keys to selling yourself. Without it, you run the risk of being perceived as disinterested or even untrustworthy.

Let's talk about the proper way to use eye contact. Eye contact is very important in two interview situations: greeting the interviewer(s) and answering questions. Unfortunately, both situations lend themselves to common mistakes, but this information will help you avoid them.

We just discussed how to greet the interviewer(s). Say your name, shake hands, and give them a greeting. Part of this systematic approach is carving out time for proper eye contact.

Nervous candidates sometimes make small, but impactful, mistakes when they are faced with several people to greet. They don't take the time to introduce themselves to each person. Instead, they hurry from one person to the next. Picture this: As I'm introducing myself to Sasha, I see that Bill is the next person. I introduce myself to her: *I'm Craig DiVizzio*, and she says her name. Next, I make a fatal mistake. I say, *Sasha, it's a pleasure to meet you*, but my body language sends a different message. What if while I'm speaking to Sasha, I'm already looking at Bill? That makes Sasha feel devalued—not a good first impression! Maintain eye contact as long as you are shaking hands and greeting each other.

Here's another common eye-contact mistake. While answering a question, a candidate may look at the person who asked the question throughout the entire answer. This approach could make the other interviewers feel devalued, distracted, disinterested, or even bored! Again, not a great first impression. A better approach is to spread eye contact among the interviewer(s) as you speak. Engage everyone in the conversation. You need each interviewer to listen and participate in the interview.

Let's talk about exactly how to distribute your gaze around the room without either staring or appearing shifty. Begin your answer by making quality eye contact with the person who asked the question. As you begin your answer, say their name. Next, distribute your eye contact around the group, looking at the other interviewers as you continue with your answer.

According to Michigan State University, one of the biggest eye-contact mistakes is staring. To remedy this, try to keep eye contact for 4-5 seconds before looking away.[4] That's about the same amount of time it takes to complete a sentence. When it's time to look away, do it slowly. Candidates whose eyes are darting around manically look nervous (or untrustworthy).

As you get close to the end of your answer, return your eye contact to the person who asked you the question. You indicate that you've completed your answer by looking back at them and nodding your head.

Have you ever heard the suggestion that keeping your gaze just above everyone's head will help you manage nervousness? Don't do this! It's rude, and eye contact is too important. If you've prepared properly, your nervousness will decrease.

If your nerves really are too much for you, there is a better strategy. At least one person on your panel will have a pleasant, smiling face. They may even nod as you speak. From time to time briefly engage with the interviewer who calms you. Once you are calm, distribute your eye contact to the others.

Using proper eye contact is essential to keeping your interviewer(s) engaged and interested in what you have to

---

[4] Schulz, Jodi. "Eye Contact: Don't Make These Mistakes." *MSU Extension*, Michigan State University, 2 Oct. 2018.

say. So, don't allow nervousness to keep you from making quality eye contact.

HOW TO SIT

Typically, how we sit is an unconscious action. Nothing could be simpler. But sitting properly requires thought. It's not the same as falling into your favorite chair at the end of a long day. During the interview, sitting properly helps establish your professional presence. It's crucial that you are aware of how you are sitting.

If you are being interviewed by one interviewer, sit facing them. For panel interviews, face the center of the group. This location allows you to engage everyone from the same distance, with just a turn of your head and maybe your shoulders.

Sit in a relaxed position—one that you can maintain for two to four minutes. Don't fumble around and jostle to get comfortable. Too much movement makes you appear nervous. Crossing your arms is a defensive posture, so keep them relaxed. Crossing your legs is fine. Position your upper body vertically or bent slightly forward (without slouching). Avoid leaning back. Leaning back makes you appear too relaxed. Remember that easy chair? That's not the look you're going for.

What about your hands? It's hard to control our hands when we are nervous. Practice how you will hold your hands when you are video recording yourself. Look for significant hand movement. Try clasping them in front of you on the desk. If that feels awkward, try placing them in your lap. If you choose to place them in your lap keep your shoulders back, never hunched.

When you review your video recordings, notice any repetitive or distracting gestures. It's okay to use hand movements when they coordinate with what you're saying, but it's distracting if your hands move repetitively for no apparent reason. For example, you may use your hands to help interviewer(s) understand your answer. You may hold up three fingers when you say, *I want to tell you three things today.*

Don't fiddle with your pen. If you're not using it, put it down. Avoid moving your hands while holding a pen. Otherwise, you're waving a wand or directing the orchestra. It's distracting.

However you choose to use your hands, keep them in the power zone. The power zone is the area below your chin, across your shoulders, and down the sides of your body. If you keep your hands in the power zone, your body is a backdrop, which keeps them from standing out.

Keep them away from the front of your face. That's distracting. Also, keep them from extending beyond the sides of your body because there's nothing behind them to provide camouflage.

Managing Your Nerves

COMFORTABLY SAYING, "I"

It's very difficult for some people to repeatedly refer to themselves. However, the interviewer(s) expect you to say *I* a lot. They view it positively because this interview is about you. If you find it difficult to say *I*, the reluctance is coming from you, not from the interviewer(s).

The only time using *I* frequently can be a detriment is if you're discussing a team project. In this situation, if you refer to what *I* accomplished and how *I* succeeded and was recognized, it may seem like you don't give credit to those deserving it. Because of this perception, some candidates use *we* a lot. Interviewers won't tell you this, but they're probably wondering what part you were responsible for. After all, they aren't hiring your team. So, here's an easy way to balance *I* and *we*. First, talk about the team assignment, what the team accomplished, and then what your role was, and how you contributed to the team's success.

First, give credit to the team. *What the team and I were able to accomplish was . . .* Then spotlight yourself. *My part in that project was to . . .* You give credit to the team for what the team accomplished, and you take credit for your contribution to the team's success. The interviewer(s) will understand your ability to work effectively on a team and appreciate your leadership as you give credit where credit is due.

COUNTERING NERVOUSNESS

Webster defines anxiety as an "overwhelming sense of apprehension and fear, often marked by physical signs (such as tension, sweating, and increased pulse rate)." The definition goes on to discuss the "threat" and "self-doubt about one's capacity to cope with [the threat]."[5] Did you notice that

---

[5] "Anxiety." *Merriam-Webster*, Merriam-Webster, Incorporated.

even Webster agrees that nervousness often results from a lack of preparation?

What if you get so nervous in an interview that it keeps you from doing your best? I have some tips for you. But first, how much and how long are you practicing? You do NOT want to doubt your "capacity to cope" with the threat.

If you have not interviewed in a long while, spend at least 60 hours preparing. Candidates hear that and think, *Really? That much*? Yes, that much because the lack of preparation causes nervousness.

Also important, if nervousness causes you to speak too quickly, intentionally slow down your speech as you practice. Practice your answers much more slowly than you usually talk. If you work on speaking very slowly, your pace will be perfect when your speech quickens at the interview.

If you can feel yourself talking too fast despite your practice, compensate by pausing briefly every now and then. Pauses after quick sentences allow the interviewer(s) to mentally process your point. If nervousness coupled with a pause causes you to forget your place in the answer, have good notes so you can glance down and find where you were.

Even if you don't typically get nervous, it could happen. Go ahead and prepare strategies to manage it. One simple strategy is to silently remind yourself that you are well prepared. You've got this. You know what you know, and your answers are good.

Finally, if your nervousness is noticeable—if your voice is shaking, for example. Simply say something like this: *Obviously, I'm nervous. Let me tell you why. This interview is important to me. I put a lot of pressure on myself to do well today because this is a job I want. I believe if given the opportunity, I'll do it well.* This statement interprets your nervousness for the interviewer(s) in a way that shows you in a good light.

Now go prepare, so your nerves don't get the best of you.

AVOIDING AWKWARD SILENCES

Cue the tense movie soundtrack. You are in the interview. You end your answer, and the interviewer stares at you but doesn't say a word. What do you do?

First, don't fill the pause by asking, *Did that answer*

your question? That's a weak and hesitant question. If you misunderstood the question or did not answer thoroughly, let the interviewer tell you. Don't ask them.

The second mistake is to continue talking—just filling the pause with too much or repetitive information. Don't ramble. Rambling shows disorganized thought.

When the interviewer is silent, often the candidate delivered their answer with uncertainty or did not indicate that they had finished their response. You can solve this problem. At the end of your answer, turn your attention and your eye contact back to the interviewer who asked you the question, nod your head, and say thank you.

On a related topic, never begin an answer unless you are sure you understand the question. It's okay to ask them to repeat or rephrase the question. Alternately, you may rephrase the question to confirm that you got it right: *Is that what you're asking?* When you begin before understanding the question, you will deliver your answer with uncertainty. It's inescapable.

Finally, know where you are going before you begin. It is okay to pause for 10 seconds, think about how you want to answer, and decide how you want your answer to end before you begin. Your delivery will sound more confident and assured. When you end your answer, nod, and say thank you.

Using these tips should manage those uncomfortable silences for you.

USING THE TIME BETWEEN QUESTIONS

Several places in the interview lend themselves to self-sabotage. One of these is the lag time between questions. This is when the interviewers are writing notes about your last answer. It could be seconds or even minutes before they ask you another question. What should you do with that awkward silence?

Many candidates don't do anything productive. They mentally review their previous answer, analyzing where they missed an opportunity or where they feel they messed up. Maybe they're watching the interviewer(s) and losing their confidence. They may worry that a lot of notetaking indicates that the interviewer(s) didn't like the answer. *I'm blowing this*, they think. This is unproductive. It's negative self-talk, and it needs to stop.

Instead of engaging in worry and negativity during this downtime, be productive and review your notes.

As part of your interview preparation, you created an interview portfolio. Your portfolio includes a methodical outline of notes for easy access. The front sheet will have a seating chart at the top. Under the seating chart, you'll have your must-say items.

While the interviewers take notes, use the seating chart to identify the person who asked you the previous question. Make an educated guess about who will ask the next question and have that name on the tip of your tongue. Remember, we said that you must communicate must-say items before the interview ends. Quickly refresh your memory. Can you cross any off? Which one do you want to try to work in next?

Your behavioral examples are also in your portfolio. Quickly review those. You only have a short time between questions, so use it productively. Don't worry about the interviewer(s). They'll let you know when they're ready for the next question.

We'll discuss your portfolio in detail later in this chapter. Make your portfolio as described and use the information effectively. The awkward silence between questions is your friend.

BUYING TIME

Regardless of how much you prepared, you may still need extra time to think about your answer before delivering it. If you practice, you can stall for time in an acceptable manner. The magic timeframe is 10 seconds. More than 10 seconds may cause the interviewer(s) to feel uncomfortable. Here are some strategies to best use those 10 seconds.

1. <u>Pause.</u>

Pause for about five seconds and look at your notes

2. <u>Will you repeat the question?</u>

Ask the interviewer to repeat the question. Even if you heard the question the first time, you can use this extra time to think about the answer.

3. <u>Repeat the question yourself.</u>

Repeat the question back to the interviewer more slowly than they asked it. For example, they might ask for an example of a time that you had a conflict with a teammate. You pause for five or six seconds, then say, *Let me make sure I understand. You're asking me to give you a time when I had a conflict with a teammate.* As you say the words, you're in your head thinking about how you will answer.

4. Write it down.

Try this: as the interviewer(s) ask the question, write it down. You may get even more than 10 seconds out of this strategy.

5. Revisit the question.

You can ask to revisit the question at the end of the interview, saying, *I'm drawing a blank right now.* Interviewers rarely have a problem with you delaying an answer—once. Only try this strategy one time.

6. Take a sip of water.

This is one of my favorites. It is a good idea to bring your own capped bottled water to the interview. It should be room temperature, maybe with some lemon or other citrus infusion. The citrus will help your voice stay clear, reducing any annoying coughing or throat clearing. Room temperature water is kinder to your voice than cold water, which can make your vocal cords tighten.

Do not take a cup of water (even with a lid). Don't accept a cup of water from the interviewer(s). An open container is an accident waiting to happen. All the interviewer(s) will remember is how you spilled liquid all over the table. *Do you remember Craig DiVizzio? He was the guy who spilled water all over the table.*

Bring capped, bottled water, only. Taking the cap off and replacing it also gives you an extra second or two. Trust me. Four, five, or even six extra seconds to consider your answer can be a lifesaver.

For your techniques to appear natural, you must practice. You certainly don't want the interviewers to think you are stalling (even if you are). Practice and deliver these techniques naturally, and the precious extra seconds are yours.

Using Your Portfolio

Part of your interview preparation is compiling a simple portfolio. You can purchase an inexpensive portfolio. It does not have to be authentic leather. The information is what's important. Allow me to outline how to set it up for easy reference during the interview.

On the left side, place copies of your references, letters of recommendation, and copies of your resume. These all fit nicely under the flap on the left.

On the right side, there is a pad of paper. On the top of the first page, you'll create the seating chart as you gather the interviewer(s) names.

In the middle of the first page, list your must-say items as bullet points. When you deliver one, cross it off. Keep it easy for you to glance down and see which ones you haven't yet delivered.

At the bottom of the first page, list your questions for the interviewers. At the end of the interview, the interviewer(s) will ask if you have any questions. It's always good to have a couple of questions. Don't worry. We'll cover what you should ask later.

On subsequent pages, list your behavioral examples. List the behavioral categories in alphabetical order and note a trigger word next to each one. The trigger word reminds you of the example situation you designed for each behavioral category.

On the last page, list questions for the greeter. Having the questions for the greeter written down is essential because you will probably be your most nervous as you are walking to the interview room. Without a written list, you may very well forget some of your questions.

Make sure the pad of paper has some blank pages for notes. Bring the portfolio and two writing pens to the interview. Over-preparation is essential!

Giving a Great Presentation

Increasingly, candidates are asked to give a presentation. Even if you don't have a lot of presentation experience, if the job requires presentation skills, the interviewer(s) have every right to see your style. Let's look at tips for delivering great presentations.

Tip 1: Use PowerPoint effectively.

Don't overload your slides with bullets. Keep them to a max of four. A best practice is to bring each point onto the slide separately. This keeps the audience from reading ahead while you are speaking. If this approach is not possible, then give them time to read the slide before you start speaking.

If you have complex graphs, try dividing them into sub-graphs. Show the whole chart and then zoom into an easily digestible segment. You absolutely do not want to confuse your audience.

Tip 2: When reading to the audience, don't move.

If you must read something, don't move. I made this mistake early in my speaking career, and no one told me about it. I saw it because I video recorded myself. As I was reading from a book, I was also walking back and forth. When you are speaking, you should move around, but reading is different because you lose eye contact. When you read and move around, it can be distracting.

Reading is a little risky anyway because you can inadvertently lose connection with your audience and even possibly lose their attention. This is because our voice changes when we read. We can't help it. So, if you read something to your audience, keep it short and don't walk around.

Tip 3: Video record yourself delivering the presentation.

Video your presentation and review it with a critical eye to see what you like about it and what you would like to change.

During the Interview

<u>Tip 4: Ask questions</u>.

Involve your audience by asking questions. You don't have to wait for an answer. The question gets them engaged. Questions allow each person to ask themselves how they would answer. When you keep your audience thinking in this way, they are less likely to get distracted or bored.

<u>Tip 5: End your presentation early</u>.

If you have ten minutes for a presentation, end at seven or eight. Ending early gives them time to ask you questions. Now, you're back to selling yourself as they larn more about you and your expertise.

<u>Tip 6: Prepare for technical difficulties</u>.

Always have back-up solutions. If your presentation is on a USB drive, save a copy to another USB drive. For good measure, you may want to store one in the cloud. Bring your laptop to the interview just in case their computer fails, is unavailable, or just doesn't work with your material.

<u>Tip 7: Bring hard copies</u>.

If time runs short, and the interviewer(s) tell you that there is not enough time for you to present, you can provide hard copies for them to review later.

Tip 8: Practice.

Practice, practice, practice your presentation!

DO YOU HAVE ANY QUESTIONS FOR ME?

If the interview is external, you need to prepare at least a couple of questions; I'll review them in just a minute. If the interview is an internal interview, you may have prepared questions, but they are not essential.

Here's a common mistake. Some candidates feel so compelled to ask a question that they ask one they already know the answer to. These types of questions are risky because the interviewer(s) may think that candidates who have done proper research should know the answer. That one may hurt you.

A less common but deadly mistake is to try to show how smart you are by asking a question to which the interviewer(s) aren't likely to know the answer. If you ask a legitimate question, and they don't know the answer, that is okay. But don't set out to embarrass the interviewer(s).

Now, let's look at some appropriate questions.

During the Interview

Questions about your first 90 days of employment are well-received and frequently asked. You may ask, *If you hire me, how would I spend my first 90 days?* Direct this question to the hiring manager. An even better version of the 90-days question goes like this: *I'm familiar with the job description, but what specifically would you want me to focus on in my first 90 days? Is there an issue or process that needs my immediate attention?*

Other questions you may ask are those that your research did not answer. You may have several of these. Plan them.

What do you do if you don't have questions because your research answered them? You can say no, but you must expand on this because interviewer(s) may expect a question. Try this: *No, I don't have questions. It was important for me to come here today knowing that I want this job and believe it's a good fit. So, I researched this job before I got here. I don't have unanswered questions. It's easy for me to tell you I want this job.* With this response, you're telling them two things. First, you are telling them you want the job. Second, you're telling them you did research before the interview, which is what they want to hear.

Of course, a final question inquires about the process.

How soon will I be notified of your decision? or *How soon will I be notified about the next steps in the process?* You need this information because you may have multiple interviews scheduled and need to plan. On the other hand, the interviewers need this question because asking it shows that you are confident that you will move to the next round of interviews.

~ 7 ~

SPECIAL SITUATIONS

Two situations require you to modify both your preparation and your delivery. The first is when you want to change directions in your career, seeking a job that is different from your current or previous position. The second is when you are clearly overqualified for the position.

Selling Transferable Skills

Maybe you need a job quickly and don't have the luxury of waiting to find the ideal job with a perfect skill match. Or maybe you aren't satisfied in your current position and would like to make a radical career change. Maybe your position was eliminated, and you are now forced to think outside the box and move your career in a new direction. Whatever your situation, the key to your success is transferrable skills.

Transferable skills are your greatest asset. These are skills acquired throughout life that can be applied to a new job or work environment. When confronting a career change, you must sell the employer on your transferable skills. Instead of focusing on your previous positions, you will focus on these skills.

To begin, use a functional resume. Almost universally, interviewers read resumes from top to bottom. A functional resume puts your skills and accomplishments at the top and moves your work history down the page. Functional resumes highlight transferable skills and

Special Situations

relevant accomplishments. The Internet has plenty of resources to help you modify your resume from chronological to functional.

Your approach in the interview will mirror this functional style. You will speak less about the positions that you've held and more about your skills and how you used them in previous positions.

When you apply for a job that is not an exact match to your skill set, you must set realistic expectations. It's a little more difficult to find an employer willing to take a chance on someone who is in a career transition.

You must ask yourself how the job you are seeking is different from your previous job. Compare the companies, the required job knowledge, and the position responsibilities. Is this going to be a minor shift, or are the two jobs light-years apart?

Take a look at the job profile and really explore the position requirements. How many of the listed skills do you have? If you don't have any, then the job may be too big of a stretch, even if you have other great skills. If you have several of the skills or at least most of the important ones, think about how you have used those skills successfully. Can you design good behavioral answers when you are asked about those skills? Can you honestly find things that cause you to be interested in the job? This realistic digging into skills and your desire is how you begin selling your transferable skills. Let's look at an example.

Imagine that an HR job requires the candidate to have recruited nurses and doctors in a hospital setting. The title of the position is Clinician Recruiter. You've never worked in a hospital, but you have recruited nurses for a business that sold computer software to home health agencies. Is this too big of a stretch? Maybe not.

Let's dig deeper. Were the nurses you recruited going to work in a hospital? No. Had the nurses you recruited ever worked in a hospital? Yes, but you recruited them to use their clinical experience to implement software for customers. Are the nursing positions different? Yes. Did the nurses you recruited and the nurses that the position expects you to recruit have different skillsets? No.

It looks like you have the skills to effectively recruit nurses to work in an environment that provides services to healthcare providers, but not specifically to a hospital. I believe there is a good chance that your recruiting skills are transferable to the position of Clinician Recruiter.

When you are selling transferrable skills, carefully formulate your answers for the interview. Design your behavioral answers to show that the skill required for the job is one you have used in the past, regardless of the work environment. Your task is to convince the interviewer that while you may not have an identical skill match, your transferable skills will allow you to be successful in the position.

To get the company to take a chance on you, you must convince them that you're worth the risk. Design your answers so that you can tell them what they cannot learn from your resume. Remember to convey your interest in the company, in the job, and in learning new skills. Highlight how quickly you've managed to learn new skills in the past.

Now let's think about a new challenge. What if the only way you can make this career change is by taking a step down. You know it will be worth the temporary set-back, but how will you convince the interviewers that you are sincere. Let's think about overqualification.

Overcoming Overqualification

Have you ever been penalized for having too much knowledge and experience? Certainly not in school, and probably not at work.

That's why it's so discouraging when you get a rejection letter for a job that asks for far less education and work experience than you possess.

Many overqualified job seekers think of themselves as a bargain that the company should welcome. Imagine getting all this experience for that wage! But the world is not that simple. I'm going to help you look at your situation realistically. When you manage your expectations, you can fight off discouragement and build on your confidence.

Let's think about someone who applies for a job for which they are overqualified. Have you ever done that? Were you desperate for work? Were you hoping to get your foot in the door so you could move up and into more desirable roles? Were you making a radical career change? Are any of those situations a benefit to the employer? Probably not.

If I'm the interviewer, and I'm reading your impressive resume, I may look at the job you're applying for and the job you held previously and make some assumptions:

- You don't plan to stay with the company long. You see this as a temporary job—when something better comes along, you'll leave. You're overqualified.
- You'll get bored with these low-level responsibilities.

Special Situations

When you get bored, you'll become disengaged. I don't need a disengaged employee. You're overqualified, and I'm suspicious.

- You must have had a nice salary in your previous job—way more than you will in this job. Eventually, you will tire of working for lower pay, so you'll leave. You're overqualified.

- I look at your resume qualifications, your lofty positions, your degrees. My gosh, you must be brilliant! You don't want this position—you want my job! You know what? You're overqualified, and I'm worried.

- I can see that you've been around for a while, doing exciting things. Maybe I don't use the word *age*, but I may surmise that perhaps you're a little stuck in your ways. I'm looking for someone I can train to do things my way. You're overqualified.

- Since you are clearly overqualified, it looks like you don't want a long-term commitment. You're desperate. You need a position with health benefits and maybe some retirement benefits as well. You're overqualified and want what we can give you. You're looking to solve your problems. You're not looking to solve our problems or contribute to our goals.

- The experience on your resume tells me that this

position is very far from your career to this point. This job is a leap. I'm going to have to spend time and money training you. I don't have extra time or money. I need help now. You're overqualified.

When you apply for a job for which you are overqualified, you have a lot to overcome. What many job seekers think is an asset can be a liability. Therefore, we must figure out how to get the interviewer to take a chance on hiring you.

First, be honest. Look at the assumptions listed above. How many of those may apply to you? If you were the employer, taking salary money out of your budget, would you take the chance?

> *Find the assumptions that could work against you.*
>
> *These are the areas that you must address.*

Take that hard look at yourself and find the assumptions that could work against you. These are the areas that you must address.

If you think the assumptions you identified may keep you from getting an interview, you can address this upfront. Use your application, resume, or cover letter to address the issue. The best way is to present the reason

Special Situations

you are interested in the position. *I am very qualified, but what excites me about your company is . . . What excites me about this job is . . .* You can mention that you plan to stay at their company for at least [*choose a time period longer than 1 year*]. Be honest. If you cannot make this commitment, don't say you can.

Now, let's imagine that your application, resume, or cover letter lands you an interview. You can address the assumptions when you meet the interviewer(s). For example, if you believe that the interviewer(s) may worry that you'll leave the company prematurely, speak about your interest in the company and how it attracted you. If you believe they could perceive you as too smart or too threatening, you can say something like this: *Yes, I have held high-level positions, and those were great opportunities, but they no longer interest me.*

Consider the following statements that take on other assumptions, but only use the ones that apply to your situation.

- *I wasn't satisfied with my last job, and I wanted a change. I'm looking for a job I enjoy, perhaps with less responsibility.*
- *I want to work on my work-life balance.*
- *I bring these unique skills to the job . . . These skills are beneficial to the company because . . .*

- *Because of my experience, I can mentor my team and prepare one or more people to succeed later in my role.*
- *Salary is important but less so for me. I have been fortunate to make good money, which makes me flexible on salary.*

You can assure the hiring manager that you aren't interested in their job, emphasizing your new interest in a better work-life balance. You can say something like this: *I still plan to work hard, but I understand the additional commitment a higher-level position requires. At this time in my career, I am interested in sharing knowledge and experience with others, helping them develop in their roles.*

Often those who are overqualified are also those who are a little older. So, we need to address the age bias. If you believe that your age may work against you, reassure the interviewer(s) that you like to work and have no plans to retire anytime soon. Say something like this: *If I enjoy this job, who knows how long I can stay and contribute.* If you can, back up this statement by referring to your long tenure at previous jobs.

Regarding an age bias against learning new things, make sure you convey how much you love to learn and how quickly you pick up new skills.

Special Situations

Another way to address the age bias is to make a point about how you enjoy good health. You may even mention any health-related hobbies you have, such as running, biking, or yoga. As a candidate, you can mention these. However, the interviewer(s) cannot lawfully ask about or comment on your health. Giving unsolicited information may encourage them to hire you.

As we know, every interview doesn't turn into an offer. So, let's look at a rejection situation. What if you get a letter telling you that you are overqualified? Send a follow-up letter to the sender. In the message say something like this: *I do have great qualifications and experience. What interests me about your company is . . . What interests me about this job is . . . What I bring to the table that others don't is . . .* Essentially, tell them that they will get more than their money's worth if they hire you because you bring skills that the other candidates may not have.

You can also try this strategy: Ask the sender or hiring manager if they are able to change or augment the position to justify hiring somebody like you. After all, you have additional skills that can benefit both the position and the company.

Finally, what if you get a rejection letter without even

getting an interview? The letter states that you were not the most qualified person. More than likely, a rejection letter will be a standard form letter with this statement, even if you did get an interview. If you get one of these, don't be discouraged. You knew you were overqualified, not underqualified. Go back and review the assumptions listed above, then tweak your resume objective, your cover letter, and your application again. Spend some time prepping your interview answers to address these assumptions as well. You'll be surprised at your success next time.

Deciding That You Don't Want the Job

What happens if, during the interview, you realize that you really don't want this job? What if you realize that the offer will be lower than you anticipated? What if their description of the position is nothing like what you imagined? Don't change anything. Keep going with your plan and everything that you've practiced.

You want them to want you, even if you think you may not want them. Does that seem like wasted effort? It's not.

Special Situations

Give a great interview. You want the hiring manager to wish he could have hired you. Such a situation could translate into getting a callback about a position that is a better fit for you. Or the hiring manager might tell a colleague who has a vacancy about you. Think of the interview as a networking opportunity. Don't burn any bridges.

Internal interviews are different. There are only two acceptable reasons for rejecting an internal job offer. One is salary and the other is a change in the position description. If the money doesn't line up correctly, you can reject the job. If the position description changed between the time you read it and the interview, you can reject the offer. You may reject a change because the job you're interviewing for and the job that was posted is not the same job.

Finally, what if the company is great, but the job turns out to be disappointing? Have you considered accepting the offer to get your foot in the door? Once you are a part of the company, you may be able to move to a job more suited to your interests.

Always give your best interview, regardless of your feelings. Putting forth your best effort is always a recipe for success.

Rejecting an Offer

Internal Offers

If you are interviewing for an internal job you must do your due diligence to avoid rejecting an offer. You never want to waste the hiring manager's time. Declining a job offer because you didn't learn what you needed to know can be a career stopper. At the very least, it can be a serious career slower downer.

To avoid this situation, gather the essential details of a potential offer in advance. For example, learn the salary range for the position, dig into the details of the job description and qualifications. You should know well in advance of an interview whether you will accept an offer.

Two situations may excuse an internal rejection: salary expectations and job responsibility changes. Let's say that you reviewed the salary range and based on your experience and qualifications, you expected to land in the middle of the range. When the offer came in, it was on the low end. You can salvage the situation by negotiating for the additional money, explaining why you think it is justified: *When I assessed this job and the salary, I* *anticipated a salary of about $5000.00 more than what was offered. Is it possible to meet that expectation?*

The other acceptable reason to reject an internal job offer is if there was a material change in the job responsibilities after you received the job description. For example, the job description lists 10% travel, but while in the interview the hiring manager says, the travel requirement is 40%. If you had this information before you committed to the interview, you would have declined.

External Offers

The two reasons listed above are also acceptable for external offers. In an external interview, you want to leave them wanting you even if you don't want them, remember? You want the hiring manager to wish you could have accepted the job. You want them to wish they could afford to pay what you expected for the position. They'll remember you and keep you in mind when another position that fits your skill set and salary expectations opens.

Always leave the interview with everybody feeling good about the meeting. Never part with hard feelings. Stick to these two rejection reasons, and you should be fine.

~ 8 ~

AFTER THE INTERVIEW

When the interview is over and you have left the interview room, you have two tasks. The first is your final etiquette matter, and the second involves preparing for the next step.

Saying Thank You

Immediately after the interview, formally thank the hiring manager and the human resources representative. It is not necessary to thank each panel member.

My first choice is a hand-written note. Choose a small notecard, one that's just large enough for a short, handwritten note, and prepare the notes in advance, omitting the salutation. You can fill that in later, after you have learned names. Before you leave the company property, ask the receptionist or administrative assistant to deliver the notes or place them in the internal mail.

With this approach, the decision-makers will receive a handwritten note within a day or sooner.

Your note should read something like this: *Dear [hiring manager], Thank you for the interview and for your time. I enjoyed meeting you and look forward to hearing from you. Sincerely, [your name]*

If you don't want to use a handwritten note, then type a letter. Put it in a regular-sized envelope. If you know the hiring manager's name, you can prepare this in advance and, as with the hand-written version, drop it off before you leave the building.

If you cannot drop the letter off while on-site, use regular mail—this should not be your first choice.

A distant third option is sending an email. Emails are easy and take minimal effort. That means they are also minimally valued. The more effort you put into your note, the more it is valued. No matter how you do it, always send a thank-you note!

Preparing for the Next Step

The next big task you have after leaving is recalling as much as you can about the interview. Do this before you start your car, if possible. You want to get your memories on paper before your mind is distracted by anything, even driving.

What questions did they ask you? Which ones did you answer well? Which answers could use some work? When you think about your performance, what do you like and what makes you anxious?

These questions will help you pinpoint what you need to change for the next time. Next time could be a follow-up interview with the hiring manager's manager. Or it could be that interview that you have scheduled with an equally great company next week.

9

OTHER INTERVIEW TYPES

As we discussed at the beginning of this book, there are several types of interviews that you may need to prepare for. You may remember that we began with face-to-face interviews because once you know how to prepare for these, it's easy to prepare for other types.

This chapter will cover preparing for the following situations:

- Internal interviews
- Virtual and prerecorded interviews
- Phone interviews
- Job fair interviews

Internal Interviews

An internal interview is an interview for a different position with the company you already work for. Most of this book has focused on external interviews, where you must learn about the company, its culture, and the hiring manager. Internal interviews have many similarities to external interviews, so you will be prepared with behavioral questions and the like. However, there are some nuances. Let's look at these now.

<u>I Want the Job</u>

First, you should already know you want the job because you had access to the job information ahead of time. It was easy for you to find out about the job, the manager, and the team. Therefore, in your introduction, tell the interviewer(s) immediately that you did your homework and you know this is the right job for you. Then, specifically explain why you want the job.

You may recall, that in external interviews, you don't say that you want the job right out of the gate. You wait until the end to avoid coming across as desperate.

For external interviews, appearing desperate forfeits your leverage in negotiations. For a refresher on how to say *I want the job* in external interviews, see the closing statement discussion in Chapter 3.

Sell Yourself

A common internal interview mistake is not telling the interviewer(s) things that they may already know about you and your work. Regardless of how well they know you, you must speak to your character and accomplishments at work. It's best to treat the interviewer(s) the same way you would treat an interviewer you do not know. Tell them everything about you. Tell them your story.

You must sell yourself and tell your story because the interviewer(s) are evaluating you based on what you say in the interview, not on what they know about you. Tell your whole story to the interviewer(s) as if you did not know them.

It can be challenging to sell yourself without sounding very formal. Here's a trick you can try: *As you know, Bill, because you and I worked on that project together, we [name your accomplishments].* When you preface your answer this way, you acknowledge that you have a history with the company while signaling that you're going to discuss your accomplishments anyway.

Meet with the Hiring Manager

Before the interview, do your best to have a meeting or at least a phone call with the hiring manager. By doing this you can not only learn what they are looking for in a successful candidate, but you can also confirm to yourself that you do, in fact, want the job. When you get to the interview, use that meeting to your advantage.

For example, when it's appropriate, turn to the hiring manager and reference the meeting: *You know, Sandy, I appreciate the 15 or 20 minutes that you gave me to discuss this position ahead of time. There was one thing that you said that convinced me this was the right job for me* . . . Referencing the meeting accomplishes two things. First, you communicate to others on the panel that you contacted the hiring manager ahead of time. You clue them in that you did your homework. Second, you explain exactly why you want the job.

References

References are less important in an internal interview than in an external interview. If you don't know the interviewer(s) at all, any additional information they gather about you will come from your references. For external interviews, make sure you review the References section in Chapter 1 again—and remember to choose excellent references.

Virtual Interviews

The virtual interview, via Zoom, GoToMeeting, Google Meet, Teams, Skype, and similar platforms, should closely reflect how you look, how you communicate, how you sound, and your body language. It should appear as if you were interviewing face to face. There is an extra challenge in virtual interviews: your space. It must appear as professional as you do. Let's look at nine essential steps to preparing for a virtual interview.

Photo by Allie on Unsplash

1. Position your computer, tablet, or smartphone so that the device camera is at eye level. Otherwise, you could appear unfamiliar with this medium, and you

Other Interview Types

certainly don't want to send the message that you are technologically challenged.

2. Sit about an arms-length from the screen. Adjust your body so that it faces the screen. This distance should put your eyes one-third of the way down on the screen, exactly where they should be.

3. The audio should be clear and free of background sounds and noises. If your device creates an echo or captures ambient noise, you may want to use a headset or earbuds.

4. Lighting should not shine down on you from above. Position lighting in front of you.

5. The area behind where you are seated should be tidy, with minimal furnishings and accessories. A busy, cluttered background is distracting. Different online platforms have different background options. Zoom allows you to use a picture as your background, but you will need a green screen (Amazon has green screens for under $50). This feature is very useful since you can take a picture of a bookcase or other office décor and still sit near your router for the best audio/visual performance. Skype allows you to blur the background. Research the media that the interviewer(s) will use. Find out what features are available and use them.

6. Keep your notes handy so that you can glance at

them when necessary. Take your eyes off the camera, glance down at your notes, quickly find what you're looking for, then look back at the screen to deliver your answer. I don't recommend using a second monitor for notes. Glancing or cutting your eyes to the side can make you look shifty or even rude. Glancing down is more natural.

7. Dress professionally. Dress exactly as if you were going to an office for a face to face interview.

8. Practice. You know by now, that I'm big on practicing. Interviewing virtually is no exception. Practice will ensure confident delivery and help reduce nervousness. Practice a virtual interview and record it. Now you can view exactly what the interviewer(s) will see and hear. Whether you use your smartphone or a webcam recorder, such as QuickTime Player or Windows Camera, record your practice interview. You will get a good check on the lighting, the background, and your microphone.

Using your recording, you can adjust whatever is necessary to ensure an optimal presentation. After you have recorded yourself, ask a friend to help you practice. Try several different platforms to make sure you are competent in each. Ask your friend to pay special attention to how you sound on each. When you get the sound right, make a note of what changes you made for

Other Interview Types

each platform.

Practice looking at the camera. If you try to make eye contact with your friend, your eyes will appear to be cast down. When you look into the camera, you are making eye-contact, whether it feels like eye contact or not. Get into the habit of looking directly at the camera. And speak slowly and clearly to accommodate any audio issues.

9. Be prepared. The day of the interview set everything up early. Make sure all systems are working correctly. You can't control a glitch during the call, but there are so many things that you can control. Set-up early and adequately. Get it all done so that you can take time to relax right before the call comes.

Final steps:

• Close any open programs on the device you are using. Eliminate any distractions. Close doors, close windows, and put the dog outside. Tell others in the house that you cannot be disturbed.

• Most virtual meeting sites have a feature that records. If you have this option, use it so that you can review the interview later.

• Sometimes, companies require you to log into their website and record answers to questions. A representative will listen to your answers later. If this happens, find and use the re-record option. Record your answer, listen, delete, and re-record until you are satisfied. Only when you are satisfied, click submit and move to the next question.

Phone Interviews

Phone interviews often precede face-to-face or virtual interviews. You must remember that in phone interviews, you no longer have the visual component. Your energy, enthusiasm, and confidence are all communicated solely through your voice. Only your words and how you say them will determine how effectively you tell your story. Therefore, how you speak your words is much more important than what you say.

There's a tried-and-true trick to delivering that energy and enthusiasm, curiosity and confidence through your voice: Stand up.

When people stand up, they sound more energetic. While standing and talking, choose a focal point, such as a painting or photograph. Instead of staring into space, you now have a face to look at. This simple tip makes the conversation more real, more focused.

Other Interview Types

Another tip is to close your eyes to block out any distractions. With your eyes closed, you can listen to your voice and vary its sound. You may speak softly at times, and then later with an excited tone. Your voice will sound magnified because you have closed your eyes and your interaction with the world—you have effectively minimized distractions.

Try it out. Make some phone calls, stand up, find a focal point, or close your eyes. Hit record on the phone and have a conversation. After the call, listen to yourself and think about what you were doing when you spoke that way. Were you standing up? Wow, that sounds good! What were you doing when your voice softened? Were you looking at a loved one's picture? Keep doing what you like and avoid what you don't.

Your goal is to project honesty, sincerity, confidence, and enthusiasm through your voice. It's a big task, so do whatever works to make it happen!

A little housekeeping tip: You must have a good phone connection. Find the best place in the house for your signal and stay there. If you move around during the call, it could cause an inconsistent or broken connection. You certainly don't want the interviewer(s) to perceive your movement. What if they think you are multitasking! Stay in one place, if possible.

As always, have your notes. Since you are on the phone, the interviewer can't see you look at your notes, so you have an advantage as long as you're careful. Use your notes, but only glance at the bullets and then look back up as if you were face to face. If you don't, you could sound like you are reading. It's easy to hear reading in someone's voice. So, use your notes, just don't look at them too long and don't read!

Just as if you were heading to a face-to-face interview, set up your portfolio several days in advance. Familiarize yourself with your notes. Know their location. Maybe the introduction and behavioral responses are on the left and the closing statement is on the right. Use a large font for easy reading.

You'll be great during a phone interview. Just prepare for it as thoroughly as you would a face-to-face interview, and you'll stand far apart from your competition.

Job Fair Interviews

There are two more interview types and I've grouped them under the heading Job Fair Interviews.

The Screening Interview

The first is a screening interview. Screening interviews often take place on college campuses. Companies generally set up tables and have brief conversations with candidates. Because of the tight job market, we're seeing more of these. They're no longer confined to a college campus, and some are even virtual.

Screening interviews last about two to three minutes. You have very little time to make an impression. The company's goal is to review your resume, ask a few questions, and formulate a first impression. This is a quick screening that narrows down the long list of candidates. From the screening, a company will decide whether to invite you to the next step in the process.

To succeed in a screening interview, communicate with high energy, and answer succinctly. Focus on your skills and your particular interest in the company. Use your 20-second opening statement.

The Mini-Interview

The second type of job-fair interview is the mini-interview. Mini interviews are a bit longer than screening interviews. They last about five to 10 minutes.

Since you have a little more time, use your full two-minute opening statement. Focus on your skills and interests that match the position. You will likely be asked some questions, so prepare some behavioral answers and some technical answers. Answer quickly, use as few words as possible and convey a high level of confidence.

10

HEY CRAIG, I GOT THE JOB

More than anything, I want to hear you say, "Hey Craig. I got the job!" So, let's review how you are going to make that happen.

First, you aren't going to worry about who has the advantage in the job market because you know that *you* have the advantage. You now know exactly how much effort goes into being successful. Most candidates don't have this information, so you have the advantage.

Because of your careful preparation, you will communicate confidence from the moment you meet the greeter. Before you answer even one question, your opening statement will have the interviewer(s) wanting to hear more.

You will have prepared not only opening and closing statements but also compelling answers to critical questions like *why do you want this job*. Behavioral questions won't trip you up because you're ready. You are prepared with a story about an interoffice conflict that shows you as a team builder and a mediator. They won't even be able to rattle you with a weakness question because you have already turned your weakness into a strength.

When other virtual interview candidates look down into their laptop camera, using a bedroom for a backdrop, you make strong eye contact with the camera in front of your tidy and soothing home office (even if it's a royalty-free picture you downloaded and projected to a green screen).

You make strong entrances and exits and use your portfolio effectively. You care so much about finding a job that fits your skillset that you sit in your car and make notes about your performance before leaving the company property. Now you are even more prepared for the next interview.

I know you're going to tell me you got the job. When you're ready to share the good news, hit me up at https://www.craigdivizzio.com/.

I'm looking forward to hearing from you!

About the Author

Craig DiVizzio has been a coach, counselor, instructor, financial planner, keynote speaker, and corporate trainer. He established his firm, DiVizzio International, in 1990, and is a motivational speaker and corporate trainer based in Atlanta, GA.

Craig's focus is on helping people develop skills to not only enhance their work, but also their lives. He's driven by his quest for excellence, passion for living, and heartfelt desire to help you become the person you know you can be.

Want to take the next step? Visit https://www.perspectives.craigdivizzio.com/ to find more DiVizzio International eLearning opportunities. While you're there, make sure to tell me, "Hey Craig, I got the job!"

One Last Thing

If you enjoyed this book or found it useful, I'd be grateful if you'd post a short review on Amazon.com. Your support really does make a difference. I read all reviews personally so I can use your feedback to make this book even better.

Thanks again for your support.